AN EXPOSITION OF EMPIRE

AMS PRESS
NEW YORK

AN EXPOSITION OF EMPIRE

BY

C. E. CARRINGTON, M.A.

CAMBRIDGE
AT THE UNIVERSITY PRESS
1947

71477

Library of Congress Cataloging in Publication Data

Carrington, Charles Edmund, 1897-
   An exposition of empire.

   Reprint of the 1947 ed. published at the University Press, Cambridge, Eng., which was issued as no. 28 of Current problems.
   Includes index.
   1. Great Britain—Colonies—History. I. Title.
II. Series: Current problems; 28.
JV1011.C3   1977   325'.341   75-41051
ISBN 0-404-14650-3

Reprinted from an original copy in the collections
of the University of Connecticut Library

From the edition of 1947, Cambridge
First AMS edition published in 1977
Manufactured in the United States of America

AMS PRESS INC.
NEW YORK, N.Y.

PREFACE

When Seeley wrote in 1883 that we seemed to have 'conquered and peopled half the world in a fit of absence of mind' he was referring, not to the method of expansion, but to the indifference displayed towards it by the educated classes. His own writings did something to remedy the defect with regard to the earlier Empire; yet later imperial history is not well known. Since Seeley's day British opinion has passed through two phases, first a period of uncritical enthusiasm for the Empire, and later a period of equally uncritical suspicion that it was not quite respectable. But what is it?

After reading Sir Ernest Barker's little book, *Ideas and Ideals of the British Empire*, I was stimulated to attempt an expansion of his theme by lightly sketching the historical background to some current problems of the Commonwealth and its dependencies. Almost everything written here is controversial and if I provoke discussion I have fulfilled my purpose.

C. E. CARRINGTON

3 *November*, 1946

Note. I am obliged to Messrs George Allen and Unwin for permission to quote from *Imperialism*, by J. A. Hobson (1938 Edition); to my wife for making the index; and to my daughter for suggesting the title of this book.

CONTENTS

Preface   v

Chapter I. What is the British Empire?   1
II. Before the American Revolution   18
III. Colonial Reform   35
IV. The Export of Men and Money   48
V. India and Africa   68
VI. Imperialism   84
VII. Anti-imperialism   103
VIII. Imperialism in Retreat   110
IX. Dominion Status   123
X. Outlook for the Future   129

Index   137

Chapter I

WHAT IS THE BRITISH EMPIRE?

The name of Empire was freely used to describe the dominions of the British Crown under the Tudor dynasty, but in a sense quite different from any we use today. The great Statute of Appeals, by which the Parliament of England threw off the jurisdiction of the Pope, begins with a magniloquent declaration in the preamble that this realm of England is an Empire and is so described in 'divers sundry old authentic histories and chronicles'. Elizabethan writers were fond of attributing to their mistress an Imperial Crown and of complimenting her person with such descriptions as 'imperial votaress'; and the full term British, or Britannic, Empire was not uncommon. James I, who was addicted to the use of high-flown language, was proclaimed at his accession King of Great Britain, a term that seems to carry an imperial connotation like Graecia Magna though it means no more than Britain in its widest sense. When, in the nineteenth century, Sir Charles Dilke named his idealized Anglo-Saxon Union Greater Britain, it was precisely an extension of Great Britain that he had in mind, Great Britain raised to a higher degree not the 'Dominion over palm and pine' that later imperialists applauded.

Even when Milton wrote of 'this Britannick Empire with all her daughter-islands about her' his vision was not ranging far afield; he was thinking of the large island Britannia with its satellites Hibernia,

Vectis, Mona and the stormy Hebrides. All these, according to historical tradition, which the Statute of Appeals had confirmed, constituted an Empire, an independent political region acknowledging no sort of subordination either to the Holy Roman Emperor or to the Pope of Rome. There was a mythical element in this theory, which was partly based upon the belief that King Arthur had asserted British independence against the Caesars and had become Emperor in his own right. The Plantagenets had exploited this belief and the Tudors, heartened by their descent from ancient British princes, held stoutly by it. Not for nothing did Henry VII give the name of Arthur to his eldest son. Remote as the fictions of Geoffrey of Monmouth may seem to be from the story of British colonial expansion they have this nominal connexion. To the Elizabethan adventurers the word Empire conveyed suggestions of Arthurian romance and the fading splendours of Rome. The extension of the notion and the application of the name to regions Caesar never knew came later in history.

When Burke wrote of the British Empire, after a hundred and fifty years of colonization, these romantic notions had been left far behind. He expressed enlightened views upon the management of a system of about twenty-seven colonies and trading posts which were bound rather loosely by a statutory commercial code known as the Acts of Trade. This organization which split apart in 1776 has been described by some historians as the First British Empire. These writers have accordingly given the name of Second British Empire to the new system which arose, in the nineteenth century from the ruins of the old. It then seemed not unreasonable, when some of the colonies emerged from tutelage into autonomy, to proceed to the next stage of nomenclature. A few political scientists, led by Professor Zimmern, have described the group of Dominions as a Third British Empire; and it has even been suggested that the Statute of Westminster marks a further stage bringing a Fourth British Empire into existence.

A chronological scheme such as this seems better suited to the monotonous procession of Egyptian dynasties than to the variegated pattern of the British dependencies. We may add, too, that the new concept of Dominion status appeared as a reaction against Caesarism. It was time to lay the ghost of the Roman Empire. The new name of British Commonwealth, proposed by Lord Rosebery in 1884, approved by Mr Bernard Shaw in 1900, adopted and popularized by the 'Round Table' Group, was given legal sanction in several state papers of the nineteen-twenties. Though sedulously used by the well informed on public occasions it cannot be said that the new name has slipped into colloquial speech, for the very good reason that no one quite knows what it means. Is India a member of the Commonwealth? Is Ireland? Is Ceylon? It appears to be the name of an ideal rather than an actual organism.

To posterity it may seem one of the strangest of English paradoxes that the purging of Caesarism from the system, the translation of the Empire into a Commonwealth, should be accompanied by a stronger attachment to the name and dignity of the King.

Should some enquirer from another world or time examine impartially this phenomenon which appears under so romantic a name, what, in fact, would he observe? It may be roughly described as a system of three concentric rings: an inner ring including the colonies of settlement, a second and larger ring including lands which have been brought under control but not colonized, and an outer ring (or rather an indefinite outer area) which may be called the British sphere of influence.

The enquirer will first discern in the creation of the colonies of settlement a complete series of events which has no parallel in human history. He will find that, ten generations ago, in the age of Shakespeare and Raleigh, the British Isles were inhabited by six or seven million people who lived upon the land and were not much noted as travellers. For lack of any better comprehensive name and without prejudice to Irish claims I shall refer to this small population and their descendants as the British Race. Their social organization was already showing signs of change and, by the end of the seventeenth century, they were becoming a nation of shopkeepers with trading interests overseas. But unlike their rivals the Dutch, whom they resembled in many ways, they also began to multiply and replenish the earth at an astounding rate. Quantitatively, by far the most noteworthy event in the history of the British Race is its increase from not more than seven million to not much less than 140 million in three hundred years. The process is now complete, since no community of British origin, excepting the 300,000 Newfoundlanders, shows a sufficient excess of births over deaths to maintain the rate of increase. No accurate census of the British Isles was taken before the year 1831 and of many parts of the world no accurate census has yet been taken. It has, however, been conjectured that the whole human race may have multiplied four or five times while the British have multiplied twenty times.

The second feature of importance in the history of the British Race is that a majority, nearly two-thirds of them, have abandoned the British Isles and live elsewhere. Our investigator, looking round for their new home, will find that these British emigrants have settled and cultivated every region in the world which was unoccupied ten generations ago, and which enjoys a temperate climate like that of north-western Europe. Such regions are not numerous; the best parts of the Atlantic and Pacific slopes of North America, Cape Colony, south-eastern Australia, New Zealand, and a few islands in mid-ocean make up the list; and all became British. In general they were sparsely inhabited by nomadic aboriginals and were settled not conquered. The other colonizing races of western Europe, the Dutch, the French, the Spanish, the Portuguese have come into possession of sub-tropical regions which can only doubtfully be regarded as 'white man's country'. In three instances only, French Acadie, Dutch Manhattan, and Dutch South Africa, did these nations occupy temperate regions, and all three came under British control.

Much of the earlier history of the colonial empires is concerned with finding the natural frontiers of white settlement. Perhaps the most striking feature of the last phase has been the extension of settlement into such areas as Texas, Queensland, Rhodesia, and even Alaska which would once have seemed unsuitable. The subjugation of the tropics and the arctic by dietary regulation and preventive medicine seems likely in the future to abolish this frontier.

History records many folk-wanderings, when races proliferate and overflow upon their neighbours, and many examples of adventurous nomadism when whole tribes transfer themselves to a land of promise. But so prolonged, systematic, and complete an extension as that of the British Race is unique in history; its nearest parallel, on a much smaller scale, is the Dispersal of the Jews. This greatest emigration could be accomplished once only in an aeon and only when capital resources, technical skill, knowledge, and enterprise were available to set the people in motion.

The population of British origin is now divided into two groups of not dissimilar size. Rather more than half, perhaps 75 million, live in the United States while rather less than half, about 65 million, inhabit what I have called the inner ring of the British Empire. Between the two groups there is this racial distinction; the British element in the American nation can no longer be separated and measured as it could be in the first census of 1790, whereas in the Dominions the British element usually holds together. The makers of the republic have adhered to the principle that their land is a 'melting-pot' in which emigrants from all the white races would be fused into a new American nation, and have so far succeeded that there is no longer an Anglo-American section. The round figure of 75 million has been reached by adding to the British element as it was in 1790 the supposed total of British emigrants between that date and 1921, and by calculating their probable rate of natural increase.

On the other hand the population of British origin in the Dominions can be calculated with a fair degree of accuracy. In Australia, New Zealand and Newfoundland, the settlers have bred true, with less foreign admixture than there now is in the British Isles. In Canada and South Africa, in spite of the efforts of many constructive statesmen from Lord Durham to General Smuts, the French and Dutch settlers have not as yet shown much sign of fusing with the British. The genius of the British Empire has worked in a contrary direction to protect and preserve the character of these minorities which are, as it were, encysted in the British organism and not absorbed. The attempt to unite Canada into a 'melting-pot' for French and British failed 100 years ago; the later system which separated the ingredients has proved to be the most successful experiment ever made in federal government. Similarly, the Union of South Africa, in spite of its name, retains safeguards for the constituent nationalities, which savour of federalism. South Africa is a potential rather than an actual Union.

In two parts of the Empire only can there be seen an equivalent to the American 'melting-pot': in western Canada where Scandinavian and Slavonic immigrants are being absorbed into the British-Canadian race, and in the West Indies where a 'coloured' race with a British culture has evolved. These exceptions go to prove the rule. The American nation, for all its devotion to a federal constitution, is in fact homogeneous and uniform. The population of the British Empire shows little tendency to mix; it is a mosaic composed of various pieces.

Unlike the inner ring of colonies by settlement, the colonies by cession and conquest constitute a political organism of a type which is quite common in history, an empire imposed upon weaker or less highly organized nations and tribes. To be sure, the dependencies (including India) annexed to the British Crown together form a more extensive, populous and wealthy area than has ever before been ruled by an alien conqueror, but it is different in degree, not in kind, from the French, Spanish, Dutch or Russian colonial empires, or from their great exemplar in ancient Rome. Although the King-Emperor stands alone among such rulers in never having exacted a penny of direct tribute from any of his provinces, it cannot be denied that the ruling race has derived many indirect profits from the British Empire; and other imperial rulers can make claims to benevolence in other respects.

The peculiar distinction of the British Colonial Empire lies in the English legal principle of trusteeship. As Sir Ernest Barker has pointed out* the contrast between the two types of colony was drawn by Blackstone. Emigrants to the settlement colonies 'carried the common-law with them' assuming with it the idea of 'a representative body having powers of taxation'. On the other hand the colonies by conquest

* *Ideas and Ideals of the British Empire*, by Sir Ernest Barker, Cambridge, 1944.

were 'subject to the free despotic power of the Crown' which meant in practice that they were protected by the rules of equity. 'If those who went out to the colonies of this order did not carry the Law of Trust with them as part of the stock-in-trade of their minds, we may say that the lawyers on the equity side, or those who were imbued with their idea of the Trust, sent it out after them.'

In the colonies by settlement there is a common citizenship in the Aristotelian sense. An Australian in Toronto or an Englishman in Cape Town finds himself quite 'at home'. Not only are the language, the laws and the administrative system substantially the same but the social stratification, the manners and habits of ordinary life, the fashions, prejudices, and amusements vary but slightly. Between one member of the Commonwealth and another the social difference is not much greater than between, say, Surrey and Tyneside. Since class distinctions have so largely been levelled away in Old England the general similarity has increased, for the Dominions enjoy the advantage of never having been burdened with an idle rich class. The unchanging features of this British way of life are instantly recognized (and often ridiculed) by travelled foreigners who hardly notice the local variations.

In the colonies by conquest or cession the British residents almost uniformly segregate themselves in order to live together in their own way. Who does not know, from his reading or experience, a number of these small societies of exiles, each with its English church and club, its tennis and tea-parties, its firm proprieties and occasional lapses, its gentility, its philistinism, and its essential honesty? Even the financial and the sexual scandals run true to type and avoid excess. Perhaps the world has never known more stable or less easily corrupted groups; their valour is to be judged by the extent and duration of their influence. Far beyond the limits of British rule these groups have penetrated, often using the accurate though confusing name of 'colony'. No true measure can be taken of the pervasive power of British civilization in the modern world without counting in these firmly defined outposts, the 'British colonies' at Shanghai, Buenos Aires, Alexandria, and at almost every other seaport in the world.

Historians have perhaps not sufficiently emphasized the overpowering predominance of British trade and finance between the Napoleonic and the German wars. Setting aside the Empire gained by settlement and the Empire gained by conquest, a third and larger Empire was gained by commerce. Through the agency of the submarine cable and the steamship, which at first were almost British monopolies, the main trade routes of the round world were opened for the first time. The export of British capital, rather than the export of British goods, started the flow and maintained the British advantage. For a whole generation in mid-nineteenth century the British position was unchallenged; and until 1914 the British led all rivals.

At every trading station in the world the British commercial colony became, more or less consciously, a centre of British culture, not because there was an intention to propagate it but because all other nations wanted to share the benefits of British industrial civilization. Macaulay's Minute on Education would have been written in vain if the babus of Bengal had not been determined to learn the language of the masters of India. In a more debased form even than babu-English the language of the nation of shopkeepers spread along the shipping routes until in all the ports of the Old World from Tien-tsin to Sierra Leone pidgin-English became the *lingua franca*. Britain really ruled the waves when half the world's ocean-going ships sailed under the red ensign and the other half was equally dependent on British cable stations, British coaling stations, and the use of a few corrupt words in the English language. All this influence was British not American, in the nineteenth century when the competition of British steamers was driving the American sailing ships off the seas, and the most enterprising Americans stayed at home to develop their own frontier lands. So far behind were the Germans when they set themselves to empire building that their officials were instructed to learn pidgin-English in order to be able to communicate with their colonial subjects.

Industrial civilization is highly infectious. All nations, from the polished Chinese to the primitive Central Africans, agreed in recognizing it as an advantage which the white men from the west should not be permitted to monopolize. The simplest savage, having once seen the technical accomplishments of the white trader and learned to converse with him in pidgin-English, can soon discover that the secret of the white man's magic lies in book-learning. And the same age that brought the trader brought the missionary. Let nothing set down here be taken to mean that I depreciate the heroism and devotion of the missionaries of other Christian sects in the great age of missionary endeavour. My concern here is not with the extension of Christendom but with the extension of British influence. Without venturing to offer any explanation of this apparent outburst of national vitality I assume that the same impulse which drove the British to extend their social and political institutions in the course of trade was also a motive force of Protestant propaganda which, in the age of expanding trade, was more active than ever before. At the end of the nineteenth century the English missionary societies were spending about £4 million a year on missions overseas. The message of salvation, the seed of the Gospel, had lain in store for centuries. It was the adventurous spirit of the nineteenth-century Britons that made them take a larger share in sowing that seed; and it was their trading connexion that enabled them to sow it far afield. The same courage, audacity and perseverance were shown by traders, missionaries and administrators alike, whether they were engaged in winning or in wasting worldly treasure. Sometimes the missionaries went first into the unknown lands since they were sure to find scope for their endeavours, while the traders were content with their market at the ports of entry.

Whatever else the missionaries achieved one thing is certain. Everywhere they founded schools at which some instruction was given in reading the English Bible. For many millions of the most intelligent boys and girls of half the world the mission school was and is the first means of approach to western civilization. There only can they learn the rudiments of literacy in the English language, the indispensable first step for the few who can aspire to technical, scientific or political progress as these things are understood in the west. In this respect the British Protestant missionaries staked out a claim for education in the English language over the most populous regions of the world, in the nineteenth century.

The history of western education in British India is too complex a subject to be discussed here, but it is irrevocable; it has left a stamp upon the minds of the Indian intelligentsia which can never be effaced by political changes. Africa south of the Sahara, if civilization at all endures, must now get its education from British schools. Modern China derives much of its philosophy, the whole of its material progress, and no small part of its woes from men educated by the Protestant missionaries. There is, however, this difference in the case of China that American missions have been as active as British. It is perhaps significant that English-speaking Liberal Protestantism has produced much the same effect upon the Chinese, whether derived from an American or from a British source. The two nations still have that degree of moral unity.

While the antagonists of empire have tended to regard the missionaries as the unconscious dupes of the capitalists, and the process of expansion as a single wave of exploitation, this is not the impression gained by most visitors to the outposts of empire. It is rather deplorable that a direct clash of interest can be observed between two classes of British residents, neither of which classes quite conforms to the Marxian rule. On the one hand missionaries and teachers together with the most progressive civil servants,* even if they do not always live up to their principles, assume that the 'natives' should, so far as possible, be treated as equals and should be brought, as soon as possible, into the family of nations. On the other hand, the traders, planters and employers of labour, the civil servants of the old school, and most military officers assume, and act firmly on the assumption, that the 'natives', whatever they may become in the future, are not yet the equals of the Europeans, and should not be treated as if they were. Ten minutes' conversation in the smoking-room of a liner will reveal quite clearly to which of these classes a traveller belongs. It is a common error among critics to suppose that the distinction is one of knowledge and ignorance, or thought and thoughtlessness, or that what we may call the left wing is purely altruistic and what we may call the right wing purely selfish; for human beings are not so neatly classified. A charitable disposition towards the 'natives' and an altruistic desire for their betterment are to be found in both classes. To act on the truism that illiterate primitives are best fitted for the simpler tasks and cannot proceed to the more complex tasks in modern society without a long period of tutelage is a quite reasonable and generous proceeding.

The problems of South Africa can never be understood without sympathy towards the Boer point of view. Their patriarchal or feudal relation to the

* Trollope noted in Jamaica in 1858 that the Governor's was the only table at which a strict colour-line was not observed.

'natives' may prove, after all, to be the best intermediate stage between barbarism and civilization. It is frequently adopted throughout the British Empire by the right wing of the colonists. The fault of imperialism does not lie here; it lies in the behaviour of the riff-raff of the settlements, the 'mean whites'—rich or poor—who think of all non-European races as inferior and ludicrous.

But I must keep to my point. While imperialism has advanced on so broad a front, sometimes with the right wing forward and sometimes with the left, it is a single advance. Rhodes and Livingstone, though their intentions seemed directly opposite, did in fact push forward the same frontier. To write down Livingstone (who penetrated farther than Rhodes) as a creature of the capitalists is too lame an explanation. The careers of both these men are parts of the same phenomenon, the irruption of British civilization, with all its good and bad features, into a more primitive society; it is a process comparable with that which planted Hellenism in Bactria and Gaul.

For the most part this frontier was advanced by the independent action of adventurers, though occasionally the Imperial Government was incited into giving its support by the pressure of some commercial group. When, rarely, the Government took the initiative by intervening from considerations of state policy its intention was almost always to protect the 'natives' from exploitation. Nothing infuriated the American colonists against the British Government more than that provision of the Quebec Act which constituted the country south of the Great Lakes into an Indian reservation from which white settlers would be excluded. Nothing antagonized the Boers so much as the setting up of imperial protectorates which limited and, as they alleged, encroached upon their frontiers. Since the seventeenth century, when the first treaties were made with the Moskito Indians of Honduras and the Iroquois of New York State, the kings and queens of Great Britain have stood in the eyes of primitive races as a remote but benevolent dynasty that occasionally intervenes to protect them from petty tyranny. The Olympian calm and unforgetting patience of the Crown have added much to the *numen* which surrounds it. Men are ruled by myths and are to be judged by the nobility or baseness of the myths they create or accept. The British may safely entrust to the judgement of posterity the myth of the Great White Queen who dispensed impartial justice, in the last resort, to so many nations through the sixty years of her reign. A cynic might object that the myth survived only because the actual interventions of the Crown (through the Secretary of State) were so rare as not to have much effect. But the power of the myth was, and is, an unchallengeable fact which endures because the myth enshrines a truth. The Crown was benevolent and, when it did intervene as from Olympus, was almost always on the side of altruistic not commercial imperialism.

A *diaspora* like the Dispersal of the Jews, a series of conquests that belittle the Roman Empire, an extension of language and culture like that which hellenized Asia: these three modes of expansion have been simultaneous. None of the three has been consistently

THREE MODES OF EXPANSION 17

pursued by any party in the state as a sustained policy. All have been the work of private adventurers under the serene lethargic patronage of the Crown which initiates nothing. In all these modes the use of the English language has carried with it certain social ideals, high standards of commercial morality, a distrust of absolute or totalitarian doctrines, law and order without militarism, comfort rather than luxury, utility rather than art. Beyond the political frontier the same notions have been diffused from cells of culture at trading-posts and missions which force nothing upon the outer world, but offer it what it greedily desires.

The benefits conferred by British commercial practice may be judged by the growth of four great cities of Asia, Bombay, Calcutta, Singapore, Hong-Kong, all of which are cities of refuge. All were neglected sites until neighbouring peoples flocked there to enjoy the blessings of British rule. Millions of Asiatics appreciated there what British energy had founded and British honour secured.

Chapter II

BEFORE THE AMERICAN REVOLUTION

This complex series of activities began, as the world knows, with the Atlantic voyages of discovery in the fifteenth century. English west-country sailors took a larger part in those expeditions than the records show; for the captains of those little ships, of rarely more than fifty tons, were mostly illiterate and, even if they kept written logs, did not write books of travel for general publication. From the specimens that industrious Hakluyt did collect we form the impression that these were samples of many similar voyages. He records one Portuguese tradition ascribing the first step in Atlantic exploration to an Englishman, Robert Macham of Bristol who eloped with a lady to Madeira of which he was the first discoverer. Certainly English adventurers accompanied their Portuguese allies to the African coast at an early date as we know from the friendly remonstrances against this interloping made by the King of Portugal to Edward IV. It was not until Protestant fervour began to depreciate the Portuguese alliance that the English began to trespass ruthlessly in this field. Joint-stock expeditions to the Gold Coast were numerous in the fifteen-fifties, and perhaps the first project to form a British settlement overseas was at Kormantin, not far from the site of Cape Coast Castle, in 1561. It failed, and no permanent trading-post was planted in Africa by the English for another hundred years.

EARLY BRITISH VOYAGES 19

The first African ventures were made in search of treasure, to get gold dust and 'olifants' teeth' in exchange for pots and kettles, steel knives, and armlets of brass wire. The traffic in slaves came later. Treasure hunting, too, was the motive of the arctic voyages towards the northwest passage. Rough old Martin Frobisher, the pioneer of these voyagers, stopped short when he found the appearance of auriferous rock; his quest, he thought, had been completed. In 1576 he made the first formal annexation of territory to the British Crown on the snowy east coast of Baffin Land. Though it was not secured by occupation it was frequently visited thereafter by English ships, and rarely by ships of other nations, so that the title has held good. Arctic Canada was thus the original province of the British Empire. Its mineral wealth which allured Frobisher (though he mistook pyrites for gold) has been established long centuries later, and Arctic Canada is the last of the undeveloped frontier-lands of promise.

From these treasure-hunting voyages north and south there emerged two valuable lines of commerce, the Newfoundland fisheries and the African slave trade. Both were supported by powerful 'interests' in the seventeenth and eighteenth centuries, cherished as nurseries of sea-power and trade by the Admiralty and by the merchants of London and Bristol. Colonies of settlement owe their origin to another 'interest', to the group of projectors who gathered round Sir Humphrey Gilbert. Their most brilliant figure was Raleigh, their publicist was Hakluyt, their most notable convert was Bacon. According to the economic doctrines of the age they proposed to extend the boundaries of empire in order to restrict the vagaries of foreign trade. A favourable balance of trade required a closed economy, since the import of commodities which could not be produced at home led to the export of bullion, a doleful prospect. But if Englishmen could be exported to the lands where these commodities were found or grown, they would exchange these exotic treasures for English manufactures to the benefit of both countries. Luckily a temporary phase of unemployment led the economists to suppose that England was over-populated and, accordingly, that emigration would ease the commonwealth.

On these principles the plantations of Ulster and Virginia were accomplished, and a large number of lesser ventures were attempted. The first, a romantic failure, was Gilbert's own expedition to Newfoundland in 1583. The issue was confused, as it was in Drake's voyage round the world, by a secret objective which is not now clearly understood. After a first visit to St John's, Gilbert sailed away on a strategic mission, from which he intended to return to Newfoundland; but was lost at sea. A vague quixotic figure, he achieved nothing, but died with a magnanimous gesture, and a phrase from *Utopia* on his lips. Newfoundland, though regularly visited by the fishing fleet, was not planted as a colony until the next generation.

It may not be amiss to enumerate the settlements of Englishmen overseas which were effectually planted in this seed time. The first was Virginia which, after several previous failures, took root in 1607. The

EARLY COLONIES

second was the colony—as distinct from the free fishery—of Newfoundland, planted by John Guy of Bristol in 1610. The third was Bermuda, inhabited by English castaways since 1609 and organized as a settlement by Richard Moore in 1612. The fourth was Surat, a 'factory' of the East India Company founded in 1613 and destined to grow into the Bombay Presidency. The fifth was the settlement of the Pilgrim Fathers in 1620. The sixth was Sir Thomas Warner's plantation of the Leeward Islands in rivalry with the French. He planted a colony in St Kitts in 1623 and later extended his efforts to Antigua and other islands. Captain Powell's occupation of the uninhabited island of Barbados, in 1625, was the seventh. The eighth was Massachusetts, begun by John Endicott in 1629. The ninth was Maryland, founded by Leonard Calvert, in 1632, on behalf of his brother Lord Baltimore. The tenth was Madras where Fort St George was built in 1641. At all of these ten settlements persons of British race have resided in every generation until the present; at six of the ten the British flag still (1946) flies.

It does not appear that the distinction between trading-posts and plantations was clear at first. The settlers were expected to draw supplies from England in the first instance, to live upon the country as soon as possible, and to concentrate upon producing a staple for export. Bacon in his essay 'Of Plantations' calls that the 'maine business', and writes with surprising liberality upon it. Perhaps we may ascribe to Captain John Smith the new conception of colonizing temperate lands where English society could be reproduced. When he found such a land he pointedly called it New England. His own colony of Virginia was a failure until it produced a staple for export—tobacco; but the New England settlements lived on their own produce and sent nothing of value to the London market. Some men who emigrated were content to act as the agents of London merchants; others went in order to live as Englishmen but in a new place. Only experience would show which of these courses would be required of them. 'The fault of our going', said Captain John Smith, 'was our own. What could be thought fitting or necessary we had, but what we should find or want we were all ignorant. Everything of worth is full of difficulties but nothing so difficult as to establish a commonwealth so far remote from men and means.' The British West Indies at first were settlement colonies cultivated by an English peasantry; later they became slave plantations for exporting sugar. The mainland colonies were a disappointment to their projectors since they led to no extension of regulated trade. However, they did 'establish commonwealths'.

One of Bacon's acute criticisms of early colonial policy was that the 'undertakers' should be 'rather noblemen and gentlemen than merchants, for they [the merchants] look ever to the present gain...the destruction of most plantations hath been the base and hasty drawing of profit in the first years'. This, with some necessary adjustments in terminology, may be a lesson for our own age. Proprietors in London took short views, to satisfy their shareholders, and approved of those colonies which paid a quick dividend. The City and the Treasury saw direct benefits in controlling

CROMWELL AND THE EMPIRE 23

Barbados and none at all in trying to control Massachusetts. Besides, the political economists had changed their tune and no longer feared over-population. After about 1630 only undesirables and irreconcilables like the papists or the quakers were encouraged to emigrate.

The interregnum is not a notable period in colonial history, but offers two useful lessons. One is a striking case of self-help in a small community when allowed liberty of action. The tiny New England settlements, quite prepared to stand alone if Old England should ruin herself with civil strife, formed and maintained a federal union which saw them through the troubled times. The other is the classic instance of the chaos caused by remote control. After Cromwell's outrageous aggression against Spain and seizure of Jamaica he attempted to plant a colony by direct administrative action from London. It was a grotesque failure which came to rights only when Charles II introduced the normal colonial system.

The later Stewart period, from the Restoration to the Treaty of Utrecht, is the great age of imperialism. A unified administration with a complete code of commercial law was formed under a permanent commission of Trade and Plantations, to control the two overlapping functions of empire. The whole system implied a comprehensive policy such as the Empire would rarely know again. In those years the main currents of imperial history were the steady growth of commerce in British ships between British ports, and the equally steady flow of emigrants to the settlements. The effect of this emigration is obvious though statistics are lacking.

About eight colonies were formed or re-formed under royal charters issued to 'noblemen and gentlemen', that is to those who by Bacon's hypothesis might be supposed to be disinterested men of honour. Systematic colonization was now better understood. Pioneers were not so ignorant as they had been when Raleigh first attempted Virginia; and statesmen at home could make better provision for the political organization. Survey and town planning got proper attention. Relations with aboriginal tribes were equitably adjusted. While Pennsylvania (1683) was the pattern of all colonizing schemes, an improvement in many respects upon Maryland and Massachusetts, it should be remembered as one of a series. Not the least interesting is the last of this group, Georgia (1732), a purely philanthropic enterprise. Though chronologically it falls in the next age it is a belated example of the High-Church and Tory philanthropy that flourished under Good Queen Anne. It now seems paradoxical that Methodism, in its earlier High-Church phase, spread through America from Tory Georgia, replacing the narrow Puritanism of New England as the characteristic American cult.

The legend of the Glorious Revolution of 1688 has its counterpart in North America where James II, before and after his accession to the throne, was actively engaged in standardizing the charters of the colonies. His intentions were reasonable enough, to reassert the authority of the Crown as the original grantor of the charters, to enforce the commercial code for the supposed benefit of all, to introduce common-law principles especially by curbing the sectarian oligarchies, and to group the smaller colonies into larger units—for which he used the name Dominion. But the colonists, like true Britons, stubbornly refused to be rationalized and fought for their old charters, illiberal though they might be. James II, accordingly, appears as a ruthless overbearing tyrant in the American as in the English history books. But, though William III moved more slowly and discreetly in his colonial policy, he moved in just the same direction, until all the offending charters, but one, had been revised. He imposed the normal form of colonial government, a royal governor and an assembly elected by the freeholders, even upon refractory Massachusetts.* In the two or three instances where proprietary government survived, it was strictly limited by the rules of common law. All colonies of settlement were then governed on very much the same principle throughout the eighteenth century. On the whole they were tranquil because they were lightly, lethargically, governed. Where an active governor attempted to use the residual powers of the Crown he inevitably provoked strife between the executive and the legislative branches of government. In some politically-minded colonies—the worst of all, perhaps, in Jamaica—the strife was chronic. A solution for this constitutional problem was not offered until Lord Durham's Report, long after the disruption of the Empire.

In another respect the policy of the Stewarts altogether failed. New England was not organized

* Almost the first act of the King's Governor was to put a stop to the witch persecution at Salem.

as a Dominion, and the Federation of the Leeward Islands was allowed to lapse. To organize the scattered colonies into larger groups for defence and commercial co-operation was too hard a task for the resources of the seventeenth century and is not easy today.

The attempt to retain the colonies within the closed economy of the old Empire by means of the Acts of Trade could not fail to demonstrate that arctic and tropical colonies were more profitable to the merchants of London than was New England. Before the end of the seventeenth century economists were beginning to ask what was the use of maintaining the New England colonies. What purpose did they serve? Virginia sent us tobacco, Jamaica sent rum, Newfoundland sent codfish, Hudson's Bay sent furs, commodities which could not easily be got elsewhere. But what did Massachusetts send that could not more profitably be produced at home?

These considerations began to tell more as the complex of interests known as 'the City' grew more powerful. Shippers, bankers, insurance agents and stock-jobbers directed an ever greater proportion of the national wealth until even country gentlemen began to venture their savings in overseas trade. Of the two rival interests, Trade and Plantations, the former prevailed in the eighteenth century and the latter took second place. It certainly did not enter into the consciousness of an age that had no accurate statistics that one-fifth of the British race already lived outside the British Isles, and was increasing far more rapidly than the four-fifths who stayed at home.

What was obvious and what was appreciated in Georgian England was shipping and sea-power, with their consequences in the shape of East Indian muslins and West Indian rum. 'Nabobs' from Bengal and sugar planters from Jamaica caught the public eye, while the drain of emigrants to the Thirteen Colonies was unnoticed. Some historians have even implied that the movement slackened after what is called the Great Emigration of the sixteen-forties though the growth of the American nation gives no support to such a view.

Trade and Plantations, the rising and the declining interest, often drew the attention of the same men in varying degrees. The 'noblemen and gentlemen' whose names appeared as proprietors of model colonies in America might also be directors of the Royal Africa Company or the Hudson's Bay Company, so that it was no easier then than now, in spite of Bacon's opinion, to separate the motives of honour and profit.

The African slave trade and the Society for the Propagation of the Gospel were typical products of one generation. The slave trade was not new and was not originated by the British; it was an established system recognized by the law of nations and turned to the purpose of the merchants of Liverpool and Bristol at this time of expansion. The two ancient missionary societies (S.P.C.K., 1698 and S.P.G., 1701) are evidence of a growing sense of responsibility towards the aboriginals in the colonies. Particular care was taken that the Indians should be justly treated at the foundation of Pennsylvania and Georgia, but perhaps the most significant advance was the protectorate established over the five nations of the Iroquois, by a series of treaties negotiated through the government of New York. In this work the missionaries of the S.P.G. were very active. The whole tribe of the faithful Mohawks were converted to Christianity in the eighteenth century and have remained the loyal adherents of the British to this day.

The Treaty of Utrecht which concluded Queen Anne's wars is the charter of recognition of the British Empire. The powers of Europe admitted England's overriding interest in the affairs of the Seven Seas. Spain, abandoning the pretence of monopolizing the New World, entered into a series of subsidiary agreements upon trade with the Spanish Main. Gibraltar was ceded as evidence of England's concern with sea-power in the Mediterranean. France renounced her territorial claims in Newfoundland and Nova Scotia, leaving the British to control the sea-ways and the fisheries. Henceforward, the Atlantic was a British ocean, which the Royal Navy would strive to defend against the world. The English people occupied both its shores and moved about it freely. Most middle-class pedigrees in England show a collateral branch in America in the eighteenth century. But those who went to the mainland colonies tended to go for good, severing their connexion with the motherland, while those who went to the West Indies kept their English contacts for purposes of trade.

England's economy after Utrecht required security for four staples: the fur trade with Hudson's Bay, the Newfoundland fisheries, the sugar trade of the West Indies, and the African slave trade. All four were based upon fortified trading-posts and upon the protection of the Royal Navy. Into this naval and commercial system the settlement colonies were expected to fit as best they could.

In rivalry with these staples, two speculative companies aroused the excitement of investors and the jealousy of independent merchants. The South Sea Company came to nothing; the East India Company after many crises rose to influence and wealth. Its early trafficking was a haphazard hunt for oriental luxuries which had to be largely bought for cash. From the beginning, though a good dividend was paid on the shares, the patronage of the directors was a valuable perquisite since the agents of the company found every opportunity and inducement to enrich themselves with dealings under the counter. No staple of trade was ever achieved until the company's servants hit upon the device of investing their current balance in Bengal opium which they sent to Canton in exchange for China tea. Thus the East India merchants lived as middlemen so far as they lived by trade. After 1765 it became more profitable to live by farming the taxes of Bengal.

It is a common complaint that the British are more ignorant than they should be of American history. This is certainly not true of the legendary tale of Washington and George III. With their curious partiality for tales against themselves, even well-informed Englishmen accept and appear to enjoy a mythical version of their own misdeeds which was largely invented by Benjamin Franklin as war propaganda, and which has long been discredited by

American scholars. What Englishmen should know, and do not, is the history of their own empire, the crisis that shook every part of it between 1763 and 1783, and the behaviour of the loyal colonies in that crisis.

The revolutionary movement was world-wide. Agitation in Boston and Virginia was conducted upon the same principles as that of John Wilkes in London, and in conscious harmony with it. The course of the struggle had analogies—perhaps contacts—with the contemporary revolution in Ireland. On the other hand, the imposition of the Stamp Act and the Tea Duties, far from being isolated and futile interferences with free states, were episodes in a sustained process of imperial reform, unlucky and ill-contrived episodes but none the less methodical and well meant. Pitt's victories in the Seven Years' War had rounded off the commercial empire of which the first design had been drawn, fifty years earlier, at Utrecht. A mounting load of debt to maintain British garrisons all over the world required a comprehensive imperial revenue. Every penny raised by the Stamp Act was to have been spent locally for the immediate defence of the colonial frontier where the redskins even then were on the warpath. The tea that was thrown into Boston harbour had been diverted there by a Chancellor whose eye roved the world to find some means of increasing the trade of Bengal. If any general criticism is to reflect upon the House of Commons, it should be that in the fateful year 1773 their attention was fixed upon remedying the real woes of India, rather than (what they supposed) the fancied wrongs of the American colonists. For the rhetoric of the Declaration of Independence should not mislead posterity into supposing that brutalities were actually inflicted on the sons of liberty in the colonies. King George had neither the will nor the means to inflict them.

The agitation against the Stamp Act was felt throughout the colonies,* but subsided when the Act was repealed; active rebellion spread from two centres, Virginia and New England. Twelve of the fourteen settlement colonies in North America adhered to the Revolutionary Congress; a thirteenth—Georgia—hesitated before adhering; the fourteenth remained stubbornly loyal. How many Englishmen are there who could give a tolerable account of the hostile Thirteen Colonies and could not name the one that was friendly?

The Revolution gained momentum in the oldest settlements where the Americans had been cut off for three or four generations from the tradition of Old England, an observation which added force to the catchword of the age, that mature colonies fall like ripe fruit from the parent tree. But even in these old provinces most estimates allow that one-third of the Americans were loyalists, and a much larger proportion among recent immigrants. Georgia and the

* In 1765 there were about 27 British dependencies in North and Central America and its adjacent islands: including Canada and three of the Windward Islands recently taken from the French; Newfoundland which technically was a 'Free Fishery' not a colony; the Hudson's Bay Company's territories; and British Honduras where the customary rights of the residents had been partially recognized by Spain. The enumeration is questionable since several groups of West Indian Islands were united for some administrative purposes, while they retained separate legislatures.

Carolinas had attracted a large number of Scottish crofters, the first of their race to migrate in considerable numbers. Though some were political refugees from the Jacobite wars, and others the victims of the earliest Highland 'clearances', almost all were loyalists in the American Revolution. It is not widely known that Flora Macdonald and her husband emigrated, and suffered for their loyalty to King George as they had previously suffered for their loyalty to King James.

On the other side the strongest resistance group was formed by protestant immigrants from Ulster. Some thousands had crossed the Atlantic in the late seventeenth century in disgust at the extension of the Acts of Trade to Ireland, and retained that repugnance when the Acts were enforced upon America. These Scotch-Irish, as they were called, formed the hard core of Washington's tiny regular army.

The main American effort was a campaign of partisans whom the British authorities quite failed to counter. As usually happens in such affairs the partisans were masters of the situation so long as they avoided pitched battles, while their adversaries were harassed and exasperated by orders based upon political speculations rather than upon logistics. After four baffling years the British Army was in secure possession of its bases, at Charleston and New York where there were many loyalists, and at the entirely loyal city of Halifax; elsewhere the country was controlled by the partisans.

Meanwhile, what had been a punitive expedition against a seditious province had grown into a world war. It was almost with relief that statesmen and soldiers turned from the hesitations, compromises and humiliations of the American campaign to an honest defensive war against the combined onslaught of France, Spain and Holland. In such a cause the nation was again united and the imbroglio in the colonies almost forgotten. When the Hearts of Oak had shown that they could fight and conquer again and again, when Rodney had punished the French Fleet off the Windward Islands and Elliot had beaten back the Spaniards from Gibraltar, the most precious parts of the Empire were safe. Let the settlement colonies drop off like ripe fruit; the fur trade and the fisheries, West Indian sugar and West African slaves were still the property of the nation of shopkeepers.

There was, however, a debt of honour to be paid. Sir Guy Carleton would not withdraw the British garrison from New York until he had provided for the loyalists who had placed themselves under his protection. Perhaps 30,000 were shipped by sea to Halifax; perhaps 20,000 went overland to found the province of Upper Canada (Ontario). Pitt spent £3 million of British money upon settling them in their new homes and gave them a constitution as like as he could make it to that of Great Britain. That, in his view, was the greatest blessing he could confer; it would save them from the abyss of republican democracy into which the Americans had fallen.

The fourteenth British settlement in America was clear of the stain of republicanism. The colony of Nova Scotia, which inherited nothing but its name from the abortive Scottish settlement made under James I and VI, had been founded in 1749 as a counterpoise to the new French fortress of Louisburg. It is an example, almost unique in British history, of a settlement colony planted by authority of the government upon a site chosen for its strategic importance. After the Peace of 1748, three thousand discharged soldiers and their families had been despatched to the site of Halifax, maintained while they first built the town and harbour works, and then settled on the land with modest advances of capital. The whole cost to the taxpayer was £415,000 over a period of seven years; and never was money better spent. Not only was the naval base fully justified in the wars, but the settlement was the nucleus about which the loyalist refugees gathered. The three maritime provinces of Canada have sprung from the seed planted at Halifax, a plain example of what can be done in the way of systematic colonization.

CHAPTER III

COLONIAL REFORM

After the defection of the Thirteen Colonies the Empire was reconstituted in the sole interests of trade secured by sea-power. Adam Smith's pronouncement, that the closed economy of the old mercantile system had been not only bad politics but—much worse than that—bad business, gradually convinced the commercial classes. It was still assumed that the staple trades must be preserved by the Navy, and conversely that sea-power must be based upon sea-traffic. But, as for America, the facts were plain; Boston and New York imported as great a quantity of British manufactured goods as when they were British colonies— nay more. Dependent as they were upon British trade (in British ships), and accepting as they did the leadership of Great Britain in science, arts and letters, they still retained many of the marks of colonial status. In the early years of industrialism, when the Americans began to import English machinery, and England to import raw cotton from the Southern States, American dependence became more marked. Even Robert Fulton borrowed the design of his celebrated steamship in Glasgow and bought the engine in Birmingham. The bland assumption that America though refractory was a colony still, was habitually made by the English ruling classes. It so infuriated the Americans as to count as one of the causes of the war of 1812, a struggle that reflects equal disgrace upon both nations.

Emigration and trade now became quite separate concerns. The disposal of the surplus population was regarded as a problem for the Home Office rather than for the Board of Trade. During the generation of wars that ended at Waterloo, while emigration was not an urgent matter, control of the Empire fell more and more into the hands of the fighting services. In 1803 a new Secretary of State was appointed, for War and the Colonies, the latter department being plainly subordinated to the former. For many years, about £3 million a year was spent by the War Office in maintaining 50,000 regular troops in colonial garrisons, which scandalized economical politicians. Pointing to the solid advantages gained by withdrawing our armies from America they asked what purpose these garrisons served, a question that became more cogent in the long years of peace. The argument that they protected the old staples lost its force as the doctrine of Free Trade slowly prevailed.

To a man of peace the Empire after Waterloo did not present an inspiring spectacle. It was a system of expensive and provocative naval and military bases to which were loosely attached territories mostly won by recent conquest. There were the old West Indian possessions (which were mortgaged, tariff-ridden and tainted with slavery); there were the captured provinces inhabited by disaffected Frenchmen and Dutchmen; there was Botany Bay; there were the territories of the East India Company whose governors were continually committing the nation to new wars and annexations. Of the scores of millions of inhabitants of the Empire overseas not one per cent were of

British race. Only two small groups of settlement colonies remained, in New South Wales and eastern Canada, and neither offered any prospect of greatness. Almost all these dependencies (excepting British India) were Crown Colonies ruled autocratically by military governors upon instructions received from the Secretary for War and the Colonies.

While Plantations were thus depressed, the growth of Trade outran all restrictions. The new colonialism which still subordinated the United States to financial and cultural control was extended to Latin America, as the states successively freed themselves from Spain with the help of British capital loans and British soldiers of fortune. The Argentine Republic was so closely associated with Great Britain by the treaty of 1825 as almost to have contracted into the British Empire. British settlers introduced sheep farming to the shores of the River Plate; British engineers built the telegraphs and the railways; British merchants imported the rolling stock; British financiers founded the banks, organized the steamship routes, built up and monopolized the external trade. The British 'colony' in Buenos Ayres was numerous enough to maintain a school, a chaplaincy, and a club in the eighteen-twenties. Most of the principal shopkeepers were British. At that time one-sixth of Britain's external trade was with South America. This was the outer ring of Empire, the sphere of influence, which enjoyed prosperity and favour; while the middle ring, the colonies by conquest, had hardly been absorbed into the system; and the inner ring, the colonies of settlement was negligibly weak.

The Houses of Parliament have always responded to pressure applied by interested parties through members who devote themselves to a particular cause. In the eighteenth century the East Indian and West Indian 'interests' had often swayed the course of politics. There had been a time when the wealth of Asia had threatened to subvert the constitution, when the profiteers known as 'nabobs' and even Indian rajahs maintained their agents in English pocket-boroughs, when all the corruption of the Ganges flowed into the Thames. The long and complex struggle over the India Bills of 1773 and 1784 and the trial of Warren Hastings purged parliament of this taint. Whatever were the faults of the Company's rule, direct political corruption was not again found in the supreme government of British India. Reverting to Bacon's old saw, Pitt determined that 'noblemen and gentlemen', not merchants, should hold the reins of government. The example set in India by Lord Cornwallis was followed by the long succession of thirty governors-general and viceroys of whom Lord Mountbatten is the latest, most of them bearers of noble names. No other such dynasty can be found in human history. There may have been indiscreet and vain viceroys, overbearing and pugnacious viceroys; not one has failed in loyalty, courage and honour, not one has used his stupendous authority for personal ends. The first and second of the line, Cornwallis and Wellesley, formed the tradition* of the Indian Civil

---

* One of the simple merits of their system was the regular payment of high salaries. Underpaid bureaucrats are always corrupt.

Service which, under the Company or under the Crown, preserved a standard of duty that Independent India will do well to maintain. When India was administered by public servants of that calibre there was little that pressure groups could do in Parliament, except at the periodical renewals of the Company's Charter (1793, 1813, 1833 and 1853).

In the early nineteenth century the West India Interest was the strongest imperial pressure group. Since the first days of the sugar trade, the importing merchants had occasionally combined for their joint advantage which did not always agree with that of the planters. Under the stress of the American War merchants and planters (many of whom lived as absentees in England), sank their differences to form the West India Committee which has a continuous history to the present day, and has never lacked representation in parliament. As Free Trade doctrines and anti-slavery agitation spread, so the more firmly did the West India Committee champion the plantation system and the preferential duties. Half the secret of Pitt's apparent coolness towards reforms had been the fact that his majority depended on the support of two antagonistic groups, the West India Interest and the Evangelicals. Later the split between these groups hastened the reform of Parliament. The West Indiamen were credited with controlling sixty pocket-boroughs so that the Evangelicals could regard a vote for reform as a vote against slavery.

The Evangelical party triumphed. Originally a small society of high churchmen and high Tories, the 'Clapham Sect', had extended their influence throughout the governing class. They obliged Castlereagh to make the abolition of the slave trade a major issue in diplomacy; they penetrated the councils of the East India Company when the devout Charles Grant became chairman; they captured the Colonial Office when his son, Lord Glenelg, became Secretary of State (1833) and James Stephen permanent undersecretary (1837). As the peace of Europe endured and as Free Trade drew nearer, strategic and mercantilist policies laguished, while philanthropy ruled in Downing Street. It slipped down from the best society into the Strand where the annual May Meetings at Exeter Hall mobilized public opinion. Evangelicalism as it became the prevailing sentiment of the age gradually changed its political colour. By the end of the century its strength lay in the radicals and nonconformists.

On 1 August 1834 the status of slavery was denounced throughout the British colonies. Young negro children and babies born after that day were given unconditional liberty while slaves of working age were transferred to a temporary status of apprenticeship. The sacred rights of property were guarded by a parliamentary grant of £20 million which was paid in cash to the London agents of the forty thousand slave owners. Most of this sum was retained by their creditors in London. Nine-tenths of the claims for compensation were settled within four years, the period of apprenticeship. A few contested claims remained outstanding until 1845 by which date the whole of the £20 million with accrued interest was disbursed. Administration of this vast undertaking cost no more than 0·75 per cent of the total fund. The number of slaves set free was estimated at 780,993 (of whom 311,000 were in Jamaica) and their value to their masters at £45 millions. In addition to the cash payments the masters had been compensated by four years' labour from the apprentices under conditions strictly defined by law. The same members of parliament who opposed the Ten-Hours Bill for English operatives forbade the planters of Jamaica to work their apprentices for more than a forty-five hour week.

This famous act of generosity, earlier in date and sounder in principle than any act of emancipation by the other slave empires, was only the beginning of England's recompense for the wrong done to the African peoples. For about fifty years, even in time of war, one-sixth of the British Navy was employed, at a cost to the taxpayer of three-quarters of a million a year, in a perpetual campaign against slave traders of less enlightened nations on the east and west coasts of Africa, regions which were drawn into the British sphere of influence. During the century of hope that followed Waterloo, the British destroyed the slave trade throughout the world by their exertions, and led the way by their example in destroying the status of slavery. When, in 1914, the lights began to go out and the shadows to lengthen across the world, it was, for the first time in history, a world of free men. There were still dark corners, even in the British Empire. Some kind of slavery survived among the primitive inland tribes of Sierra Leone, the colony founded by the Evangelicals, until as recent a date as 1924; but such nooks and crannies of barbarism were rapidly being cleaned out. Two or three Oriental states retained their customary domestic slavery in a rather shamefaced manner, and that was all. When the British record comes up for judgement at the bar of history, they may rest their case upon the administration of India and the abolition of slavery.

In no way can the retrogression of the world towards barbarism, since 1914, be more clearly seen than in the modern attitude towards slavery, one of those heavily-charged words that are used most often in a rhetorical sense. The name of slave brings to the mind's eye the picture of a wretched half-naked negro 'beside the ungathered rice', the victim sacrificed to a Simon Legree and saved by a Lincoln or a Wilberforce. When we read of the African slave trade we shudder at the insensibility of our parents and thank God that we are better men. There are three degrees of guilt in slave mongering. The first is the simple cruelty of the slave raider who preys upon his own species, hunting human beings as other men hunt hares. 'Can you stop a cat from mousing', asked one such emir. 'When I die you will find a slave in my mouth.' This— let us allow ourselves the credit—has not been a British national sport. When some rogues began to practise it in the western Pacific, under the name of 'blackbirding', the news called forth general indignation. The second degree is the calculated brutality of the legalized trade in human merchandise, for long years the perquisite of the men of Liverpool and Bristol. To do them justice it should be remembered that it paid the traders best to keep their livestock healthy; a nation of animal lovers could be trusted to see to that. The third degree is the callous tyranny of the slave master who lives with his human furniture and despises it. While men can tolerate the sight of other men used as chattels the guilt of slavery is not yet expiated.

A hundred years ago the British race underwent a moral conversion. The cause of personal liberty, not for themselves alone but for others also, inspired our Victorian grandparents to renounce human property of their own, and to defy, threaten, cajole, bribe, or overthrow the oppressors of human beings elsewhere until, as they supposed, they had banished slavery from the world for ever. It has crept back, not into darkest Africa but into white men's countries. Through all those lands where totalitarian governments have ruled, the seizure of political opponents and their assignment to forced labour without legal protection has been the common practice of the last thirty years; and no voice of protest is now heard from Exeter Hall. The torch that enlightens the world today is no longer held in the hand of Liberty.

When the Evangelicals had freed the slaves they next turned their attention to the native tribes in the colonies. The sciences of ethnology, anthropology and comparative religion were still unknown. The aborigines of newly discovered countries were regarded as innocents living in a golden age, capable of immediate social progress if carefully introduced to civilized practices and Christian morals. Unfortunately, it was much more plain that they were capable of acquiring white men's vices and dying from white men's diseases. To the Evangelicals the choice of paths lay open, to salvation led by the missionaries, or to damnation led by the traders in rum and fire-arms. A parliamentary commission came down strongly on the side of the missionaries in 1837, recommending that colonial governors should take advice upon native affairs from the missionaries, and that missionaries should be appointed as protectors of the aborigines. Though the findings of the committee were not embodied in legislation they were taken as rules of guidance by the Colonial Office. The secretary of the Church Missionary Society was now the confidant of Sir James Stephen. Two favourite fields of missionary endeavour were Cape Colony and New Zealand. In both the Colonial Office was urged to set up protected native states, free from contamination by trade or settlements, so that the missionaries could organize them as Evangelical Utopias.

While the Sugar Interest and the Missionary Interest were contending over the body and soul of the negro, the settlers in New South Wales and Canada crept back into public notice. They now attracted attention because the Malthusian school of economists had again raised an alarm of over-population. Emigration as a cure for unemployment was a popular theme for academic exercises by writers at the time of the new poor law until, from a chaos of barren theories and misbegotten plans, the creed and practice of the Colonial Reformers emerged.

Thirty or forty years ago the general reader knew little or nothing of the Colonial Reformers whose achievements were hardly mentioned in the popular histories but, as Lord Durham foretold on his death-

THE COLONIAL REFORMERS 45

bed, posterity has done justice to him at least, if not to the others of his set. His associates were not a pressure group but a devoted band of students and publicists, like the Fabian Society. Durham died young, leaving no successor of political eminence to dominate the group. Charles Buller, the brilliant pupil of Carlyle, was their link with parliament, John Stuart Mill their philosopher, Rintoul of the *Spectator* their press agent. Many young radical politicians and some young Tories took up colonial reform. When Mr Gladstone was taxed in old age with being a Little Englander he would boast that in the 'forties he too had sat at the feet of Gibbon Wakefield, the eccentric personality about whom the Colonial Reformers moved. Wakefield was at the back of every colonizing scheme for thirty years.

The story is now pretty well known of this man of fashion who, when serving a sentence in Newgate for the abduction of an heiress, beguiled his time by studying prison reform, transportation, convict colonies, and finally what free colonies might be. The Wakefield Plan instantly became the norm of colonizing theory. Colonists and administrators were for it or against it, tried to implement or to modify it, but could not ignore it. The Colonial Office adopted the plan in part, in 1831, and for the next twenty years it was the common form of colonization, though never exempt from the harshest criticism. Its author's bad record hindered the reputation of his schemes. An impetuous, quarrelsome, secretive man, he fell foul of all his associates though they could never dispense with his advice. When he died in New

Zealand, in 1862, his work was forgotten and his grave neglected.

Wakefield was an economist—he edited Adam Smith—and his name was known for theories of land tenure. Yet he never lost sight of the fact that the art of colonization is not a device for draining off the surplus of population, nor for developing the export market; it is concerned with begetting new societies which must justify their own existence. His plan was simple; he would work wonders in a new country by charging a high price for land. A raw community has one asset only, one factor of production—the land, and that should not be squandered. To the land there must be applied labour and capital in due proportion, since either without the other is helpless. The ratio could be adjusted only by adjusting the price of land, in order to prevent settlers from monopolizing more land than they could use. Thus population would be concentrated, and 'concentration means civilization'. Instead of scattered ranches producing a cash crop for capitalists overseas, the settlers would form a closely knit community with the comforts of social life and the prospect of stabilizing their economy upon a home market. Capital would be attracted and commerce would grow.

This practical device was only half of his programme. He first pointed out that a respectable society needs a proper balance of sexes. Emigrants should be selected and a preference given to young married or marriageable persons. Nor would settlers of the right sort be attracted to a colony without amenities which (as this was the nineteenth, not the twentieth, century) meant churches and schools. The best colonies, as in the days of Penn and Baltimore whom the Colonial Reformers loved to quote, would be organized by religious bodies. But Penn and Baltimore, said Wakefield, would never have gone to America to be governed by remote control from Downing Street according to the whims of the Colonial Office. Without entire self-government, such as the American colonies had enjoyed two hundred years ago, systematic colonization would be a mockery.

When Lord Durham went to Canada, taking Buller as his political secretary and Wakefield as his adviser upon land settlement, a new struggle began between the Colonial Reformers and the Missionary Interest. The Reformers would gladly have come to terms; they did all in their power to assure the Evangelicals that their planned settlements would not injure native interests; but the missionaries were implacable. The advent of Lord John Russell's government in 1846 was a victory for the Colonial Reformers since Henry, Earl Grey, one of their number, became Colonial Secretary. He established Responsible Government, as recommended by Lord Durham's Report, in Canada, the Maritime Provinces, Newfoundland, and in four Australian states.

Chapter IV

THE EXPORT OF MEN AND MONEY

In the five and twenty years that followed the grant of Responsible Government, the British nation dominated the world by its wealth, scientific attainments, technical skill, expanding population and adventurous spirit. Perhaps no historic myth is more wildly at variance with the facts than that which represents the mid-Victorians as a stuffy and complacent generation. The richness of British eccentricity has never been so apparent as in the days of 'Rajah' Brooke, Richard Burton, Bishop Colenso, 'Chinese' Gordon, Governor Eyre, John Nicholson, Francis Galton, Winwood Reade, Waghorn of the Overland Route, Dr Livingstone and Shepstone of Natal, to take a few names at random. From the great proconsuls like Sir George Grey and Sir Bartle Frere down to the buccaneers and beachcombers like Ross of the Cocos Islands, and 'Bully' Hayes of the Kanaka Trade, these Victorians share two common qualities and two only, their stark courage and their violent individualism. They were to be found in almost every land and sea, often quite alone among peoples who seemed manifestly inferior because the Englishman everywhere dominated them. Outside the English-speaking countries the travelling Englishman was able to demand the respect due to wealth, power and character. The first two would not have assured his position had not the whole world known what was meant by

BRITISH PIONEERS

palabra ingles. Rarely has any one nation so patently led the march of progress; never before had any master race imposed itself by the action of individuals who went their way without the least reliance upon government support. For better or worse, half the world in the later ninteenth century was moulded to the British pattern. Not only India and Egypt, but Latin America and even China, more or less deliberately, began to take the same shape. All the world was then the sterling area.

The British race excelled in sheer vitality. The pioneers and adventurers were the precursors of a wave of migration from the British Isles that reached its highest crest in 1852, but ran on until 1914 fluctuating rather than slackening. The export of men has been less studied by historians and economists than other branches of overseas traffic and cannot be statistically treated since the evidence is insufficient. A sketch of the broad effect can, however, be attempted.

The old Empire was English rather than British. An analysis of the American census of 1790 gives the origin of 70 per cent of American citizens as English, 8 per cent Scottish, and 9 per cent Irish (mostly Scotch-Irish). The Catholic Irish had not then begun to emigrate in large numbers. These early emigrants had been sturdy adventurers from the middle classes and the peasantry, of whom many had crossed the sea at their own charges with a reasoned hope of bettering themselves. Not a few had been inspired by high ideals of founding or adhering to new model commonwealths. Such an assumption must not be pressed too far, since the early colonies also received batches of refugees, paupers and convicts who were unlikely to settle as good citizens; yet, on the whole, it was a superior section of the community that emigrated and, on the whole, the emigration was voluntary.

Between 1815 and 1840 about a million persons abandoned the British Isles, half of them for British North America. Of these a large majority were flying from distress, because they must go, not because they wished to. And they were largely escaping from Scotland and Ireland. The depopulation of the Highlands began with the pacification, when chiefs no longer kept a fighting 'tail' of idle clansmen. Johnson remarked in the Highlands, in 1773, that all the talk was of emigration. 'The lairds', he said, 'make a wilderness of their estates. Instead of improving their country they diminished their people.' Thirty years later the clearances were much worse though no one in authority, except Lord Selkirk a lowlander, made much protest. It is an ironic commentary on the romantic legend of the north that the very chiefs who revived the tartans, the pipes, and the kilted dress, who luxuriated in the glow of the Waverley Novels, were engaged at the same time in destroying the clans and driving away their kin. But Scotland's loss was Canada's gain and the highlanders were not frail plants that languished when uprooted.

No traveller in the Empire can fail to notice how high a proportion of the leaders of colonial life are Scottish, especially the doctors and the engineers. This Highland predominance is first to be observed among the traders of the far north-west in the seventeen-nineties. There were also many group settlements, whose history has not been recorded for the general reader. The character of these emigrants, and the difficulty of giving statistics of emigration may be exemplified in the story of the Waipu Highlanders.

A party of McLeods from Sutherlandshire migrated to Cape Breton Island but did not prosper there. In 1851, their leader, an aged minister, ordained a further migration on the advice of his sailor son who had seen the world. One hundred and thirty of them set off in a barque which they themselves had built and, after trying South Australia, moved on again to Waipu in New Zealand. Several more shiploads followed making a colony of 900 souls whose descendants still spoke Gaelic in the twentieth century.

The story of the depopulation of Ireland is strangely different. As Wakefield bitterly said, 'the Irish do not colonize; they only emigrate miserably.' Though a peasant people at home, they become town dwellers when they go overseas, constituting the mass of unskilled labourers in the cities of America and Australia, while Scotsmen everywhere find their way to positions of responsibility.

A wave of emigration, or rather of refugees escaping from distress, began, about the year 1820, from Ireland to North America. At first the rural slums of Connaught were merely decanted into the urban slums of Montreal and New York in conditions of wretchedness which were denounced in Lord Durham's Report. Later, although the flow was strengthened, the intake was rapidly absorbed because, of all emigrants, the Irish did most in the way of family self-help. An Irishman would no sooner begin to draw wages at the high colonial rate than he would plan to send for his family and friends and to pay their passage from his savings. Thus the migration gained momentum. But the Irish rarely pioneered, unless soldiers of fortune are to be called pioneers, and never founded new settlements; they followed as proletarians in the last stage of colonization.

Flight from distress, a feature of the Hungry 'Forties in all three kingdoms, became precipitate after the Irish Famine. Flood tide was reached in 1851, when a gross figure of 336,000 persons, 257,000 of them Irish, left the British Isles. Although the rate of natural increase was high the total population of Ireland fell by more than 40 per cent in fifty years. In the same years the population of England was doubled although emigration from England also stood at a high rate, averaging about one-quarter of the natural increase. Thus the population movements of the 'forties and 'fifties quite altered the balance of the English, Scottish and Irish nations. Ireland in 1841 contained nearly one-third of the population of the British Isles; in 1931 it contained less than one-tenth. Substantially the Irish race now lives in America with a small minority in Ireland and a not much smaller one in the Dominions. The Scots, too, have largely abandoned Scotland,* but for the Dominions rather than America.

In England also the name of Emigration recalls to the labouring classes a faint memory of the Hungry 'Forties, a suggestion of misery and exile, though there

* These general statements do not allow for the internal migration of Scotsmen and Irishmen to England. A simple test of the frequency of typical surnames in books of reference implies that there are many more Scots in London than in Edinburgh.

was never a general exodus like that of the Irish and the Scots. The aristocracy, who did not emigrate, disdained the colonies as 'low'. Political economists (other than the Colonial Reformers) treated the subject in terms of disposing of the unemployed, and radical politicians sang to the same tune. An active prejudice against emigration long survived in the left wing of politics, where it was always seen as a means of getting rid of the unwanted not as a means of providing the lucky with a splendid opening. Such narrow views may be studied in the parliamentary debates of 1935,* when the House of Commons paid this important subject the rare tribute of a little attention.

Undeterred by this stream of misinformation the sober industrious classes provided a steady flow of adventurous colonists. Thomas Pringle described a section of them in his account of the '1820 Settlers' in Cape Colony. Thousands of honest families were selected to form the nucleus and set the tone of Wakefield's six planned settlements in Australia and New Zealand. Early visitors remarked upon the difference between the human material in these and in other raw societies. Wakefield wrote of his favourite Canterbury, not without a touch of irony: 'I would have fancied myself in England but for the hard-working industry of the Upper Classes and the luxurious independence of the common people.'

The Canterbury Settlement of 1850 was the most complete and, on the whole, the most successful of all

* See for example the speech of Mr Aneurin Bevan (*Hansard*, 18 December 1935) against 'the proposition that we ought to push people overseas'.

British colonizing schemes. It enjoyed the advantages of wide publicity and enthusiasm, the blessing of the Archbishop, and the patronage of *The Times* newspaper. When the first party of settlers, 750 persons of whom 120 were 'gentry', worshipped together in St Paul's Cathedral before sailing, it was felt that the great age of colonization had returned. No colony was ever planted without miscalculations and setbacks, which were not lacking in New Zealand. Some of the more romantic dreams which the Canterbury Settlers indulged in were not realized for thirty years or more, but within seven years a decent thriving agricultural community of 7000 souls* was well established and self-supporting, having repaid the sums advanced by guarantors for unforeseen expenses. In 1858 Canterbury was reputed to be one of the most prosperous societies in the world. It was perhaps rather overloaded with schoolmasters and clergy. With this last and best of colonizing experiments the tradition of Penn and Baltimore, sad to say, was allowed to die.

The critical years, 1846 to 1852, which saw the adoption of Free Trade by Great Britain, the grant of Responsible Government to the Colonies, the great emigration, and the final attempts at systematic colonization were also remarkable for the two most celebrated discoveries of gold in history. The luck of the 'forty-niners in California gave the necessary fillip to the emigrants whom pressure of population was already driving westward. The pushing out of the American frontier became a rush for a golden prize.

* The Canterbury block now sustains not much less than a quarter of a million inhabitants.

Though few of the amateur prospectors enriched themselves the wealth of the world was immediately and permanently increased. A new state or colony was born at each goldfield through the simultaneous appearance of fresh labour and capital. Many goldfields had a mushroom growth which vanished when the 'pay streak' gave out, but many grew into stable societies. The top of the boom in California was hardly passed before the news of gold in Victoria brought the second of the world-wide gold rushes to Melbourne in 1852.

Let experts in the science of currency calculate the effect of a huge expansion in the circulating medium at a time of apparent over-population and folk-wandering. To what extent either was the consequence of the other, to what extent either or both stimulated the progress of steam, the building of trunk railroads, and the organization of shipping lines: all these are open questions. Historically all were simultaneous and logically all must have reacted upon one another.

The gold rush doubled the population of Australia (400,000 in 1850; 1 million in 1860) but did not change its essential character. Though the people of Sydney abandoned even their annual race-meeting to flock to the Turon field; though the Governor of Victoria was left in solitary state because his servants and even his police had run to the diggings at Bendigo, the wool trade and the squatters* were the gainers in the long

---

* It may be necessary to remind readers in 1946 that the term 'squatter' usually referred in the last century to flock masters who occupied large tracts of grazing land in the colonies, without firm title.

run. Victoria was inflated by the production of gold from a small and struggling pastoral colony to a great and rich pastoral colony. The gold finds in New Zealand had a similar effect there. The beneficent providence that beamed upon British endeavour in the nineteenth century led the prospectors to 'payable' gold in each dominion in turn, so that each was given its opportunity of expansion. After the Australian finds of 1851 in New South Wales and Victoria there followed the rushes to the caribou country of British Columbia in 1858 and to Gabriel's Gully in southern New Zealand three years later. In 1867 came the Gympie Rush to Queensland. A variant on the theme was the opening of the diamondfields at Kimberley in 1871. Many smaller finds of gold in Africa preceded the striking of the main reef deep below the Rand in 1894. The Golden Mile at Kalgoorlie in Western Australia boomed in the same year. Last came the Klondyke rush of 1897 which first pointed out to Canadians their destiny 'down north' in the arctic.

Not all resembled the original gold rush to Melbourne, where the settlement resumed its original character after the diggings were worked out. At Kalgoorlie and Johannesburg the first spontaneous phase of the gold rush, when individuals washed out dirt in tin pans and swapped packets of gold dust over the counters of saloons, was soon succeeded by mechanized mining which required heavy capital investment and an industrial community. Australian and South African capitalists both experimented with coolie labour and both rejected it. In both countries the white mining community made efforts to preserve the mines for white labour, a feeble and momentary effort on the Rand but a powerful and sustained effort by a great majority of the people in Australia. In Africa the sons of Ham were destined to be servants to their brethren while in white Australia the 'digger' was to be master, the national type.

The goldfields were not lawless places though they were rough. The most striking feature of the 'Forty-nine in California was not the violence and lynching but the spontaneous democracy that reacted against it, in a land with no legitimate government. Customary miners' law was respected and was enforced by elective vigilance committees. Vice and corruption flourished at the 'wide open' cities where the lucky spent their money, but not at the diggings, where claim jumpers and gold stealers got short shrift. The miner, with his slouched hat and moleskins stuffed into long boots, his prominent six-shooter, his generosity, his addiction to gambling, and his roving habits was a hard manual worker. When his luck turned he easily became a wage labourer, but did not lose his radical democracy, nor his jargon—of staking claims, and making lucky strikes which panned out badly, ending in a washout which left him stony broke. All these mannerisms and characteristics became the common form of the emigrant, the guise he assumed to prove himself no longer a tenderfoot. The prospector or mining engineer was the typical pioneer of the later nineteenth century; the democratic 'digger' was the typical emigrant. Socially the types were quite different from the drovers and the land-hungry farmers' boys of the earlier settlements. All early theorists on the subject of colonization thought and wrote in terms of agriculture. 'Unlocking the Land' was the slogan of advanced politics in the Dominions. Land hunger was the motive of most emigrants who, when they secured their land, became natural conservatives. But the colonist as miner was a very different man from the colonist as settler.

When Englishmen spoke of 'the colonies' in 1830 their minds turned naturally to the West Indies; when they spoke of 'the colonies' in 1880 their minds turned to Australia where gold was the lure and wool the staple of production. The five Australian states, excluding Western Australia and New Zealand which developed on independent lines, satisfied every criterion of colonization: by exporting a raw material, wool, for which there was an increasing demand in England; by importing British manufactures at a rate of £10 per head of the population per annum; by accepting a steady stream of British emigrants; by dispensing with garrisons of regular troops; and by giving the Colonial Office very little trouble. The lucky incidence of the gold finds coming just at that stage of their history where capital investment was required, placed them on a sounder financial base than most new countries so that they were not hampered by external debt. It was not until about 1883 that the Australian colonies began to borrow heavily on the London market. All were coastal settlements whose communications went by sea and whose development was not obliged to wait upon the construction of expensive trunk railways.

No other new nation has so smooth and comfortable a history as Australia in the nineteenth century. It suffered none of those massacres, frenzies or reigns of terror that make the story of other lands so attractive to the arm-chair critic. The nearest thing to a battle was the democratic outbreak at the Eureka Stockade, where a dispute over gold miners' licences led to a fight in which four soldiers and thirty miners were killed. So steady was the progress, so easy was the social life that J. A. Froude, who was in Melbourne in 1885, ventured a prophecy that Australia would be the last refuge of the English landed gentry. There they would be able to live as they wished, 'without fear of socialism or graduated income-tax', which were likely to be the ruin of Old England. He was even then behind the times. The colony of Victoria was already deeply committed to the doctrines of David Syme of the *Melbourne Age* who advocated, at that early date, a form of state socialism with a completely planned economy based upon high wages, protection for secondary industries, and strictly limited immigration. Until the financial crash of 1894, protection seemed to have insured Melbourne's prosperity. The reason for the long delay in federating Australia was Sydney's unwillingness to adhere to these new-fangled economic heresies. Sir George Reid, the popular premier of New South Wales, said that for a free-trader like himself to join with the protectionists of Victoria would be like 'a teetotaller keeping company with drunkards'. In the end he lapsed from his principles, and the Commonwealth came into existence as a planned economy with a prejudice against immigration.

The common form of colonization in Australia and New Zealand may thus be summarized. First came planned settlements on the coast; then the occupation of the hinterland by squatters on pastoral leases; then attempts by radical governments to 'unlock the land', that is to resume Crown rights over the pastoral 'runs' in order to sell the land to agricultural smallholders at a fixed price. The sums realized by land sales were used for subsidizing the import of selected immigrants. In several settlements successively the inflation caused by a gold rush raised wages, introduced immigrants of a different character, and led to a demand for secondary industries and protection.

Very different was the history of Canada, the Tory Dominion. Development, from early days, was directed by big business and dependent upon imported capital. It might hardly be too much to say that the whole story of British Canada might be written round the magical groups of initials, 'H.B.C.' and 'C.P.R.' Canada, like Russia, has a perpetual economic problem, to find an outlet from the heart of the continent to icefree oceans. Canada's dilemma whether to link her economy southwards with the United States or eastwards with Great Britain, whether to be a continental or a thalassic state, was solved for the nineteenth century by the railway builders who attracted first the Maritime Provinces and later the Prairie Provinces into the orbit of Montreal and Toronto, by railways running east and west, railways which were built, equipped, maintained, and for long periods run at a loss, with the aid of British capital.

The third limb of the British exporting business, the

export of capital for investment, began to dominate the world even more than the export of men or manufactured goods, as the Hungry 'Forties gave way to the comfortable 'fifties and well-fed 'sixties. It was only during the Napoleonic Wars that London had succeeded Amsterdam as the market where money was always available for foreign loans. For many years this form of business was quite private and quite speculative. Neither Castlereagh nor Canning nor Aberdeen nor Palmerston thought it any part of their duty to guarantee loans of British money to foreign powers, much less to use diplomatic pressure for recovering bad debts. Reconstruction loans to continental powers after Waterloo whetted the appetite of investors who began to look farther afield in the eighteen-twenties. About £20 million, a large sum for those days, was rashly invested in loans to revolutionary juntas in Latin America. In general the shareholders lost their money, though the banking houses flourished on commissions. Mr Dombey considered that to break one's heart on account of an adverse speculation in Peruvian mines was 'a very respectable way of doing it', provided that Dombey and Son grew rich by floating the loan. The only permanently productive advances of that period were made to the Argentine and backed by treaties of reciprocal free trade which were vastly beneficial to both countries for a hundred years.

After the South American boom of the 'twenties came the North American boom of the 'thirties which broke at the banking crisis of 1837. Most of the £30 million advanced to various states of the Union by London bankers was lost. Two states, Michigan and Mississippi repudiated their debts finally and absolutely. American credit sank so low that agents of the Federal Government failed to raise a loan anywhere in Europe, on any terms. 'Not a dollar', said Rothschild. By comparison with these large undertakings the sums invested in projects for colonial land settlement were small change.

The next decade saw the beginning of the railway boom which reached its height in England, in 1846; and spread from country to country throughout the rest of the century. In no other respect did British leadership stand out so prominently as in railway construction which brought to a head all the humours of the Victorian age. London, alone of financial centres, could advance the money; the engineers of Scotland and the north country far surpassed all others in technical skill; England and Ireland could bring forth armies of 'navvies', the aristocrats of manual labour, ready to migrate anywhere and drive cuttings or raise embankments of more than Roman grandeur. Britain exported the rails, the locomotives, and the rolling stock, and could export the coal for driving them. British trade to the country opened by each new line would, sooner or later, justify the outlay. Thus railway loans were a solider investment than the speculative political loans of the previous generation. Current politics in many new countries became a struggle between pressure groups for railway concessions to this or that new area which was reported ripe for development. The heroes of the age were the railway builders, brave, hearty, full-blooded pioneers who moved in the margin between politics and finance, a field of social activity where the union of theory and practice was perfect. All the world agreed that steam locomotion was the very type and glory of the Victorian age, and the men who organized it were the directors of beneficial progress; all agreed, that is to say, except a handful of Pre-Raphaelites and poets.

Greatest of the railway contractors, greater even than the two Stephensons, was Thomas Brassey who undertook 170 contracts for 8000 miles of railway in five continents between 1840 and 1865. He employed 80,000 men sending them abroad in organized parties with teachers, doctors, and clergy. Four thousand British navvies worked for him on the Paris-Rouen railway alone. His was solid productive work quite unlike the bubble finance of the earlier forms of foreign investment; he even survived the great crash of Overend Gurney's in 1866 which brought down so many railway financiers.

But the monopoly was too rich to last. Under the Second Empire Napoleon III began to tempt the savings of the frugal French out of the proverbial stocking and into railway enterprises of his own; and no sooner was peace restored after the American Civil War than the wealth of the United States began to tell in the international investment market. From year to year the Americans were less dependent upon importing British machinery, better able to finance their own expansion, more inclined to invest their occasional surplus of capital overseas. Germany appeared as a third competitor after 1871. As the Utopian dream of the free-traders faded, protective tariffs, strategic railways, and guaranteed loans became the dominant factors in international politics. Capital loans for national development by means of trunk railways were advocated by colonial statesmen of the new school and, belatedly, the 'City' turned to the colonies as a field for investment.

The Grand Trunk Railway of Canada, an all-weather route from Montreal to the sea at Halifax, was financed by loans raised on the London market with a guarantee from Lord Grey at the Colonial Office. Barings raised the money, £12 million in all; Brassey built the line, which never paid its way in sixty years. In fact, its purpose was strategic and political, not commercial. By linking the Maritime Provinces with Quebec it induced the recalcitrant province of Nova Scotia to throw in its lot with the Dominion.

When the secret history of the last century is written the part played by the firm of Baring Brothers in consolidating the British Empire will be made conspicuous. Their timely arrangement of a loan of £2 million to the nascent Dominion clinched the arguments over confederation at the Westminster Conference of 1867; and their negotiations with the Hudson's Bay Company brought about the conveyance to the Dominion of the Company's territories. Baring Brothers acted as bankers to the Dominion for many years, but publicly and privately the Baring family were engaged in wider imperial concerns. Neither Howards nor Russells can show braver honours than the progeny of Johann Baring, a Lutheran pastor's son who came from Bremen to London to seek his fortune in 1717. The pastor's grandson Francis Baring, whom

Pitt made a baronet was the greatest merchant banker in the world, the 'sixth great power of Europe'. His sons, grandsons and great-grandsons, who intermarried prudently among the aristocracy, were promoted to five peerages, so that the common reader knows them better under the noble names of Ashburton, Northbrook, Revelstoke or Cromer. One of their number was ambassador to Washington, another was Bishop of Durham. One was a Whig and another a Tory Chancellor of the Exchequer. One was Viceroy of India, another was High Commissioner in Egypt. Two or three Barings were prominent in the Colonial Reform movement and figure in the correspondence of Gibbon Wakefield. A talent for management and negotiation was hereditary in the individuals of this family; and the influence of the family firm was always applied to strengthening the colonies by productive investment. When the House of Baring came to grief in the financial crisis of 1890, it was the end of the age of private banking.

The beneficent influence of Barings in the background of Canadian affairs should not divert the reader's attention from the practical idealism of the Canadian leaders; for the confederation of Canada was a triumph of statecraft. Sir John Macdonald was a thick-skinned, unscrupulous partisan, but a man of long views and broad sympathies. Are we to admire more his concept of the scattered French and British settlements as a nation which could and should be united, or the tactical skill with which he combined conflicting interests, or the persistence with which he overcame the apathy of Downing Street? He would have made

Canada a kingdom united to Great Britain only by allegiance to the Queen if he had not been thwarted by the Colonial Office, where it was thought that the Americans might take offence at the royal title. The alternative, a Dominion 'from sea to sea' was proposed by Sir Leonard Tilley of New Brunswick.

The puzzle of Canadian confederation is to account for the behaviour of Joseph Howe of Nova Scotia, a veteran loyalist, who rallied his province at the last moment against absorption into the Dominion. To plead his cause in the House of Commons he raised up John Bright the Radical, who saw fit to add to his brief on Nova Scotian separatism some unworthy sneers against Canadian loyalty, a malignity which might well be forgotten if it were not the only debating point made by any English statesman upon the British North America Act. It was taken in the House, said Macdonald, as if it were an administrative measure for uniting three parishes. At least one Canadian delegate returned to Canada convinced that both Gladstone and Disraeli were disappointed because Canada had not seceded from the Empire.

Yet the British North America Act of 1867 was surely the chief constructive measure of that parliament. As the fundamental statute of the Canadian polity it stands almost unamended after eighty years, during which the British constitution has been altered out of all recognition. Federalism, with Lincoln just dead and Bismarck riding roughshod over the German states, was then in bad odour; but the Canadian statesmen at the Quebec Convention devised a federation far more workable than the American Republic or the

German Bund, and neither Germans nor Americans had so difficult a problem to solve. They were not confronted with 'two nations warring in the bosom of a single state', and nations radically opposed in language, laws, religion and social organization. Granted that the federal union of the two Canadas was but a *mariage de convenance*, the surprising fact is that the partners have got along together pretty well, succeeding where Dutch and Belgians, Norwegians and Swedes, Hungarians and Austrians have failed. Assessing the difficulties and considering what has happened elsewhere in these last three generations the British North America Act may well claim to be the most successful written constitution in history.

CHAPTER V

INDIA AND AFRICA

Politicians at home cared little for Canada and the public hardly got wind of events there. That residue or *detritus* of history that lingers as folk-lore—'1066 and all that'—preserves no record of the founding of the first Dominion. Only one imperial event in mid-Victorian times, the Indian Mutiny, fired the imagination of the British public. In an age of liberalism the sudden return of hideous violence, with its revelation that massacre could provoke even British soldiers to bloody reprisal, came as a psychological shock. The treachery at Cawnpore was never forgiven; the reprisals were explained and excused. It ended the prospect of sympathy and co-operation between Indians and British throughout Bengal and the United Provinces.

It may be worth while to pause and recapitulate the stages by which British rule had been extended over India. After the servants of the Company had secured control over the administration of Bengal the province was at first exploited with not much more show of justice than had been displayed by its former rulers, until Warren Hastings gave it an honest, efficient administration, and Cornwallis gave security of tenure by making the landlord class responsible for the land-tax.

Southern India came into British hands as a side-issue of the French wars. The long struggle for sea-power in the Indian Ocean inevitably embroiled the French and British commanders in combinations with ambitious Indian princes. At one time the adventurers who usurped the throne of Mysore seemed likely to make southern India into an independent Moslem state but, siding with the French, they were involved in the general ruin of the French colonial empire. The capture of Mauritius in 1810 put an end to French power in Asia and left the British paramount. Since that date the old Madras Presidency, with its three satellite states, each as large as some European kingdoms, Hyderabad, Travancore and Mysore (where the legitimate dynasty was eventually restored by the British), have enjoyed almost unbroken peace. This great region for a hundred and forty years has been the happy country that has no history.

The third phase of the British conquest was the suppression of the Marathas, a confederacy of Hindu princes who might have fostered a Hindu national revival to end the anarchy then prevailing in central India, but who preferred to live by rapine and predatory war. Once committed to the government of large parts of India, the British were obliged to come to a *modus vivendi* with adjacent peoples; but the Marathas knew no other way of life than warfare either with their neighbours or among themselves. The pacification of central India, completed by about 1823, took the form of creating several defined principalities for these warlike chiefs, and of liberating several Rajput principalities from Maratha tyranny. These Rajput states are the oldest legitimate governments in India.

The way was now clear and the time had come to confer upon India the blessings of western progress. 'Victory may be inconstant to our arms', said Macaulay with sublime confidence. 'There is an Empire exempt from all natural causes of decay, the imperishable Empire of our arts and our morals, our literature and our laws.'* The new era of enlightenment set in when Lord William Bentinck on the one hand, and Ram Mohan Roy on the other, attempted a synthesis of eastern and western liberalism. If the British gave India a western education and a western penal code, they also revived Sanskrit classics and investigated ancient history which the Hindus themselves had forgotten. Indian nationalism itself was a by-product of western education in the English language. The unity of India under a single sovereign government was first achieved by Lord Dalhousie whose conquests extended farther than those of Asoka or Akbar. He planned the roads and railways which for the first time made it possible for these territories to be brought under one administration; he also gave India its first university.

Dalhousie had inherited from his two predecessors an empire newly balanced by accessions of territory in the north-west. British foreign policy in the eighteen-thirties and 'forties had drawn India into a new strategic contest for world power, in which Russia had succeeded France as England's rival. Lord Roberts once pointed out how strange and unforeseen was the convergence of Russian and British aggression towards the Khyber Pass. In 1700 the Russians at Orenburg

* House of Commons, 10 July, 1833.

and the British at Fort St George were 4000 miles apart and hardly aware of one another's situation. In 1850 when the British held the Punjab and the Russians had reached the Aral sea the distance separating them had shrunk to 1000 miles; in 1873 it was no more than 400. By this time the rivalry was evident. The two empires drew together by alternate and competitive bounds as a glance at an historical atlas will show. The methods of both were similar, though the Russians were inclined to defend their policy with pretence and bluster, while the British preferred excuses pitched in a highly moral tone. The motive of economic exploitation had little to do with these advances into the barrens of central Asia. Each step forward was an act of what is now called power politics, and on both sides the cautious intentions of diplomats in Europe were often expedited by the audacity of accredited or unaccredited or discredited agents on the frontier; for considerations of prestige made it difficult to recover a false step. The disastrous Afghan campaign of 1839–40 was a setback to the military reputation of the British which was by no means restored by the punitive expedition of 1841. While many Moslem amir-ates were annexed or converted into protectorates, either by the British or the Russians, the Amir-ate of Kabul was allowed to continue as a buffer state though it was of no great antiquity and deserved no more consideration than Bokhara and Quetta which were annexed. By the year 1885 it had been squeezed and moulded into its present shape as the kingdom of Afghanistan.

The secret history of the partition of central Asia is not to be found in the annals of the Colonial Office or of the Board of Trade, hardly even in the India Office. It was a facet of the eastern question and a concern of the Foreign Office. The three functions of the Victorian empire, export of men, export of goods, export of money, hardly touched it. But the consequent wars were entailed upon British India and profoundly affected its development.

When the British first showed the flag in the north-west they appeared as allies of the Sikh nation against their hereditary enemies, the Pathans. It was foolish pugnacity on the part of the Sikh leaders, after the death of the wise old Runjeet Singh, that impelled them to invade British territory and challenge the British to battle for the lordship of Hindustan. The three Sikh wars were quite unlike earlier Indian campaigns in respect of the severity of the fighting. The Sikhs behaved with the courage and tenacity of a European army and came near to beating large forces of British infantry in fair fight. They failed, and submitted gamely to the fortune of war.

The new province was lucky in providing scope for the boldest individuals of an unsurpassed generation. The high sense of duty, earnestness, inflexible justice, unflinching moral courage of the mid-Victorians were exemplified in the men who 'took over' the Punjab, especially in the three Lawrence brothers. There was something in the air of these healthy wheat-growing plains with their virile peoples that drew the sympathy of the British, something that they had not found in crowded feverish Bengal. The British *raj* renewed its youth in the north-west and redoubled its self-confidence. Kipling's India, the land which the *sahibs*

LORD DALHOUSIE'S ANNEXATIONS 73

ruled with an unshakable sense of responsibility, was the Punjab; and the civilians and soldiers from the Punjab saved British India in the Mutiny.

Economic and administrative progress in the new provinces—the whole tendency of the age—encouraged Dalhousie to take every opportunity of reorganizing the worn-out relics of ancient monarchies as efficient modern provinces. Like a medieval autocrat he sought to make the Crown every vassal's heir. The 'doctrine of lapse' by which he justified the annexation of five or six feudatory states, when their rulers died without leaving sons to succeed them, was most salutary from the aspect of good government; never more salutary than in the case of that byword for misrule, the kingdom of Oudh. But the pace of reform was too fast and, when a military mutiny broke out in the Bengal army, there were sympathetic stirrings in many other quarters: against the innovations that broke caste rules, against the influence of Christian missionaries, against the replacement of lax and corrupt government by honest and strict government.

The Mutiny did not spread far, perhaps because no revolutionary leader, nothing resembling a hero, arose among the sepoys. The mutineers spent their force in mere tumultuary anarchy, some dreaming of reviving the Mogul Empire under the king of Delhi who was a nonagenarian, others of reviving the Maratha power under a luxurious sadist known as Nana Sahib. On the other part no hostile critic of imperialism could deny to the men from the north-west who stayed the Mutiny the virtues of courage, leadership and loyalty. But, while admitting that the British few again asserted their superiority in martial virtues over the Indian many, it should be remembered that Sikh volunteers from the Punjab formed the bulk of the army that suppressed the Bengal sepoys. That comradeship-in-arms between the British and the warlike races has lasted a hundred years through many trials. Though commonly neglected by ideologues it forms as genuine a link in the chain of Indian unity as some others which nowadays are more approved, but have not been tried in the fire.

The blood shed in the Massacre of Cawnpore, and in reprisal for the massacre, cried out from the ground. The British who formerly had appeared as the rejuvenators, almost as the liberators, of India were again reprobated as a conquering caste. They drew apart, imposing their innovations upon a sullen people. The Queen's Proclamation assured the Indians that their religious beliefs and practices, however repugnant to evangelical opinion, would not again be tampered with. There was a change, too, in the course of political influence. All the earlier wars had been against Indian dynasties which were conceived to be potential rivals of the British *raj*; the Mutiny, so far as it ever took shape, was a class war, a rising of the military caste against its commanders. In this class war the greater princes, the Nizam, the Maratha and Rajput chiefs, supported the British Government. Thereafter they were its allies, at once the supporters and the dependents of the Queen-Empress.

The heroic age of personal rule by men who made their lifelong careers in India, and mostly died there, passed into the new age of efficient management by

INDIA AFTER THE MUTINY

bureaucrats; who lived withdrawn from their subjects; who brought out to India the *memsahibs*, a class more exclusive even than the *sahibs*; who maintained their home ties by steamer trips backwards and forwards through the Suez Canal; who were always tethered to Whitehall with telegraph wire. India was now held in trust and was to be governed as the trustees thought best for it.

In the age of expansion that continued until the slump of the late 'seventies, hardly any practical man of the world doubted that railway construction and Free Trade would bring prosperity to India, or that material prosperity meant social progress. Looking backward it may appear that what was called Free Trade amounted to the destruction of Indian arts and crafts by underselling their products with cheap and nasty cotton goods and other manufactured articles. A shipping monopoly, and railways subsidized by the Indian taxpayer, helped the British exporter.

About £14 million of British capital had been invested in Indian railways before the Mutiny, to the satisfaction of the shareholders who observed that the price of stock kept pretty firm. The pacification of 1858 was followed by a boom in trade when India at last began to export raw materials in bulk, making a start with cotton during the scarcity caused by the American Civil War, and proceeding with rice which first appeared in English nurseries in the eighteen-sixties. Accordingly English investors came to regard the Indian Empire as a profitable field for investment, so that, by 1870, about £150 million was committed there, half of it in railways. The safeguards intended in Dalhousie's original plan, for limiting Indian liability, for controlling costs, and for ensuring that railway concessions would eventually revert to the state, were gradually whittled away by the moneyed men and the *laisser-faire* economists, in spite of the protests of John Lawrence. The interest on guaranteed railways loans was always a heavy burden on the Indian revenue, making a substantial part of the 'home charges', that drain of cash payments from Calcutta to London which critics of British rule have denounced as a concealed tribute. India, however, got an excellent railway service, far superior to any other outside western Europe and the United States.

British commerce, and public works produced by British wealth and skill, should, according to the optimists, have raised the standard of life of the Indian people; but that standard remained obstinately low. The life of the peasants, holding land under settled tenures and cultivating crops for local consumption, was simply regulated by the Malthusian Law. Irrigation of land led to a great increase of population; peace and order enabled a larger number to survive; the railways made it possible for the *sahibs* to organize famine relief* and so to remove the severest check upon natural increase; the Indians multiplied and remained poor.

Indian railway finance was one of the problems bandied back and forth between Gladstone and Dis-

* Note that the periodic famines of the old days in India were caused by local failures in some particular crop. The Famine Code compiled in 1883 upon experience in other years of scarcity solved the problem of distribution between fat and lean provinces. It could not feed the hungry in a famine like that of 1943 when the shortage of food was absolute and world wide.

CAPE OF GOOD HOPE

raeli in the 'seventies; another was provoked by annexations in South Africa. Until 1870 no English Government could be persuaded to regard South Africa as anything but a useful strategic harbour with a worthless and troublesome hinterland:

> 'the Cape whose ill-starred name,
> Long since divorced from Hope suggests but shame,
> Disaster, and thy captains held at bay
> By naked hordes'.

The only pressure group that could stir the Colonial Office to action there was Exeter Hall which made itself the patron of the 'naked hordes' and persistently denounced the Boers as their oppressors. The missionaries were held responsible for abolishing slavery on terms which the settled Boers of Cape Colony thought unjust, for insisting that the Hottentot servants of the *trek-boers* should have legal equality with their masters, for throwing the mantle of British protection over Bantu tribes with whom the 'emigrant farmers' beyond the Orange river were at war. Missionary interference and Whitehall vacillation convinced the Boers that they might despise and should mistrust the policy of the British Government.

Whitehall divested itself of all responsibility for those Boers who had trekked north into the wilderness beyond the Vaal, and of almost all responsibility for those who had remained nearer at hand between the Vaal and Orange rivers, though these latter emigrants included many Englishmen. And having divested itself, the Colonial Office proceeded to harry the emigrants with criticisms of their native policy. The Orange Free State, the little farmers' democracy that grew up round the half-English settlement of Bloemfontein, at first bore no malice against the British settlers and retained the closest connexion with the Cape. In fact the Free State protested against being driven out of the Empire.

When Sir George Grey, that phoenix among colonial governors, got the hearty concurrence of the Free State in a plan for federating South Africa, the obvious solution of the problem, the Secretary of State shrank with horror from the suggestion, and recalled Sir George Grey in disgrace. The Colonial Office continued to hold aloof in theory and to interfere in practice.

In the central highlands of South Africa sat the wisest of all Bantu chiefs, Moshesh of the Basutos, after resisting British and Boer attacks upon his stronghold. He shrewdly saw that only British protection could save his land from Boer conquest and at last, in 1868, the Colonial Office was persuaded to announce a protectorate over Basutoland. This was the first of the modern protectorates which so enormously increased the extent of the Colonial Empire between 1869 and 1905. It infuriated the Free State Boers who regarded it merely as aid and countenance given to their savage enemy.

Not many months later Gladstone's government struck the Free State a harder blow, when diamonds were discovered near its unmarked western frontier. A rush to the diamondfields, both of white nomads from the diggings in other lands and of Kaffir labourers in search of high wages, had the usual inflationary effect upon the peasant economy of Bloemfontein. It was

ATTEMPTS TO FEDERATE SOUTH AFRICA 79

not surprising that expansionists at the Cape should advance a claim to this disputed territory on behalf of a Griqua chief who was supposed to be a British subject; but it was surprising that a government over which Mr Gladstone presided should support this flimsy claim. The diggings were annexed and renamed Kimberley after Gladstone's Colonial Secretary. Too late, a judicial enquiry was held, at which the Griqua's claim was demolished but the wrong done to the Free State was not righted. Compensation for the annexed territory was paid to the amount of £90,000, a handsome addition to the petty revenue of the Free State but a derisory sum when balanced against the wealth of the diamondfields. This deplorable piece of sharp practice blighted the fortunes of South Africa. Until then, in spite of many blunders and signs of weakness, British policy had been directed on the whole to the altruistic protection of native rights; thereafter it never got back to the strait path but was frequently deflected by unworthy intrigues.

When Disraeli came to Downing Street, his Colonial Secretary, Lord Carnarvon, a well-meaning but rather inadequate man, was convinced that he could heal the wounds of South Africa in the same way as those of Canada had been healed. He remembered that he had steered the British North America Act through parliament. But the Cape politicians were lukewarm about a scheme which would burden them with the cost of maintaining the penniless hinterland, and it was hopeless now to expect co-operation from the outraged Free State. The habit of annexing provinces for their own good was, however, growing upon the Colonial

Office, and not a dog barked when Carnarvon sent an emissary to annex the bankrupt disorderly Transvaal province where handfuls of wandering Boers were seizing territory left and right without respect to the claims of native tribes.

Carnarvon's trump card was sending to the Cape a tried imperial statesman, a scholar, a churchman, and a man of the world, who was to do for South Africa what Durham had done for Canada. He came too late and, though he won the respect of all parties, Sir Bartle Frere could not calm the universal unrest. When the soldiers mismanaged the Zulu War he was held responsible and was dismissed by Gladstone who just then returned to power. A magnanimous policy might have reconciled the rival races but Gladstone, after provoking the Boers by declaring that he would not withdraw from the Transvaal, changed his mind under pressure. When the Transvaalers declared their independence and defeated a small British column in a skirmish at Majuba, he gave way. A grant of self-government before Majuba, with a guaranteed loan, would have established the Transvaal as a contented state. The British negotiators were, however, instructed, after Majuba, to hedge round the retrocession of the Transvaal with not less than fifteen irritating limitations, and to haggle over the last penny of the financial terms on which they would do what they admitted to be their duty. The one factor slurred over in this sordid bargaining was the interest of the British loyalists who were given no protection, a sorry contrast to Pitt's vindication of the American loyalists in 1783.

The Boers, who previously thought that the British cared for nothing but humbug, now thought that they cared for nothing but money. They were not surprised at a revived British interest in the Transvaal when the finds of payable gold on the Rand suddenly converted the backward little republic from the poorest to the richest community in the world.

Chamberlain disdainfully wondered what there was about South Africa that made all its politicians into blackguards. But it was Gladstone's first government that annexed the diamondfields, and his second that hemmed in the Boer republics on the west by setting up a protectorate over the Christian Bechuanas. Mere blackguard conduct would not account for all the twistings of policy in the Free State and the Transvaal, at the Cape and at the Colonial Office, among the missionaries and among the moneyed men.

The downward path led inexorably into the abyss of the Boer War by way of Rhodes' bid for control of Bechuanaland, his occupation of Rhodesia, the diplomatic struggle with Germany for ports on the southwest and south-east coasts, the Uitlander agitation, and the Jameson Raid. To the Boers the whole sequence of events seemed to be explained by the British lust for gold. Even Smuts once thought that they might be bribed, by the cession of the Rand, into leaving the rest of South Africa to the Boers. In fact both parties were equally corrupted by gold. Kruger, like Rhodes, proposed to use the wealth of the mines to further his political ends. He would have created a Dutch South Africa from which all forms of British influence would be excluded; and, if necessary, he was fully prepared to use force. A far more pathetic tragedy than the clash between Rhodes and Kruger was the alienation of the Orange Free State, a rural democracy bound by many ties of commerce and friendship to its British neighbours. Here no baleful influence of high finance or of indentured labour poisoned the social organism. The tide of industrial progress flowed past Bloemfontein to the storm centre of Johannesburg, leaving the farmers of the Free State in resentful isolation. The Afrikaner literary and political revival, the *Sinn Fein* of South Africa, came to its strength under Hertzog in the Free State, not in the rough mixed community of the Transvaal.

All the varieties of British colonial policy may be seen in the pattern of South African affairs during the 'seventies and 'eighties: emigration, trade and investment; altruism and avarice; protection of natives and industrial exploitation; indirect rule of backward peoples, grants of self-government to white communities; mean encroachments and generous withdrawals; the Colonial Office in its arbitrary and overbearing mood, the Colonial Office dilatory and negligent; a microcosm of empire. It will not be necessary for my purpose to trace a continuous thread of narrative beyond this point. The Empire had taken its shape and set its course for about forty years, the climax of its greatness.

The British nation lived by exporting its surplus of men, money and goods. The earnings of the emigrants and the profit of the overseas investments provided the nation at home with a far higher standard of life than could have been attained by the mere exchange of goods for goods. This happy state of affairs, an economy that continually expanded, though the rate of expansion fluctuated, lasted as long as the surplus of men and money lasted.

At those points to which the flow of men, money and goods was simultaneously attracted for developing the natural resources of virgin soil (as in Canada, Australia and New Zealand), the effect was permanently beneficial to the old country and to the new. Where the flow found its way to an already populous dependency, whether to an ancient civilization like that of India or a barbarous society like that of Rhodesia, there appeared a phenomenon which is now harshly criticized under the name of 'imperialism', a short, limited, and accidental phase in British history. Few instances can be found where the desire to find a new field for investment was the efficient cause of 'imperialist' annexations. Throughout the period the broadest flow of men, money and goods and of the social influences they carried with them, was neither to the white dominions nor to the colonial dependencies, but to foreign lands. In spite of the efforts of the imperialists who would have directed the flow, the doctrine of Free Trade prevailed. Whereas the goods that went to foreign countries might be exchanged for goods, the capital that went in foreign investments has been largely squandered. Far more serious was the outward flow of emigrants who were lost to the family of British nations for ever.

Chapter VI

IMPERIALISM

It might be supposed that the arrival of the whole imperial organism at maturity in the eighteen-sixties would have stirred an outburst of enthusiasm but, such was the sentiment of the age, this climax was neither approved nor even noticed by statesmen and philosophers. The principle of *laisser-faire*, carried to the bounds of anarchism, so dominated English thought that no constructive measure got much attention. Material progress was assumed to depend upon breaking down barriers and removing constraints. Nothing else was much approved, nothing else was much attempted in politics in the days of Gladstone's first administration. The tone of imperial thinking had been set by Cobden who spoke of 'the colonies, the army, the navy, the church, and the corn laws, merely accessories of our aristocratic government'. The corn laws had gone but, he thought, it would take fifty years of the antiseptic effect of Free Trade 'to purge these impurities' from our constitution altogether. Since the Tories had accepted Free Trade no party in the state took any other view of the imperial future. It was the realization of this universal indifference that so disheartened the Canadian delegates in 1867. At the Colonial Office itself, which had shrunk into a minor department when the War Office was separated from it during the Crimean War, the 'Little England' doctrines were strongly entrenched.

Two successive under-secretaries acted and spoke publicly and privately, as if they were engaged in winding up a dissolved partnership. The colonies had got self-government and could enjoy the blessings of Free Trade with Great Britain. Now let them go in peace. Sir Henry Taylor, when under-secretary, went so far as to inform the Governor-General of Canada that he thought that province a *damnosa haereditas*. He deplored the improved relations with Canada as 'the worst consequences of the late dispute with the United States'.

A puny counter-blast against this general attitude was delivered by a group of obscure men, many of them colonials living in London, who founded the Royal Colonial Institute in 1868, as a centre for information, on the model of the Royal Geographical Society. It had no party affiliation, and Gladstone was a guest at the inaugural dinner. Some of those who were brought together at the Colonial Institute, notably Sir George Grey and J. A. Froude, formed an active group for bringing pressure on the government. They harried Gladstone and his Colonial Secretary by inciting questions in parliament about the withdrawal of British troops from New Zealand before the Maori wars were won, and about the Government's emigration policy.

Lord Granville had made it clear to the New Zealand Government, not without some good reasons, that he washed his hands of the Maori wars; and went further to imply that he would be glad to wash away all connexion with New Zealand of any kind. Did Mr Gladstone positively intend to disintegrate the

British Empire? To this question the Prime Minister gave an obscure and evasive answer. Grey and Froude presented a petition signed by 100,000 workmen asking whether Mr Gladstone would assist them to emigrate to a British colony. Mr Gladstone would not. Froude prophesied against the Government in the monthly journals, pointing out, in vain, what now seems hardly worth pointing out. *Laisser-faire* policy had reached such a stage that a Liberal Government no longer accepted any responsibility for the people of England: they were free to starve, or free to go away at their own charges; and if they went away no one cared where they went.

There was, however, a diplomatic problem in the background. The bulk of British migration was towards the United States where newcomers were made welcome. Gladstone's foreign policy turned upon the necessity of improving British relations with the United States, to which end he was ready to appease the Americans by any means in his power. He would overlook aggressions committed by Americans against Canada;* he would pay any sums in order to settle the Alabama claims; and he would certainly not divert the flow of emigrants to a British colony lest the Americans should regard it as an unfriendly act.

A best-seller of the year 1869 was Dilke's *Greater Britain*, a book full of acute observations on the Anglo-Saxon world but strangely faulty in its judgements. The author naïvely assumed that the moral reunion of

* It should be remembered that American filibusters made unprovoked aggressions against Canada in 1812, 1838, 1866 and 1871.

England and America was inevitable, and regarded the colonies as an obstacle in the way. Why, he asked, should we provide an army to protect the French-Canadians, who hated us, against the Americans who ought to be our dearest friends? What return, he asked, could we expect from the colonies; adding, with irony which the course of history has strangely reversed, that 'Australia would scarcely feel herself deeply interested in the guarantee of Luxemburg, nor Canada in the affairs of Servia'?

Canadian interests were sacrificed in the negotiations over the Treaty of Washington, 1871, to the dismay of Sir John Macdonald, the loyalist premier. With difficulty he persuaded his parliament to accept the terms. But, taking a longer view, we can see that Gladstone's policy was, in the main, justified. After 1871, Anglo-American relations steadily improved, to the advantage of Canada as well as of England.

The pin-pricks of the colonial champions had more effect upon the opposition than upon the government. Disraeli, who had shown not the slightest sympathy for the colonies in the first sixty-five years of his life, shrewdly grasped at this new weapon of offence against Gladstone. In 1872 he announced that 'the Liberals view everything in a financial aspect, totally passing by those moral and political considerations which make nations great. The colonies have decided that the Empire shall not be destroyed'. The new electorate, enfranchized five years earlier, consisted of working men who knew more about the colonies, through their brothers who had emigrated, than did the 'noblemen and gentlemen' in Downing Street.

A ripple of imperial enthusiasm swelled the wave that floated Disraeli into power in 1874; and there the matter rested.

There is little justification for the legend that describes Gladstone as the enemy and Disraeli as the apostle of empire, since neither gave the subject much attention. But for the acquisition of the Suez Canal shares Disraeli's imperial policy consisted mainly of large florid gestures. The forward policy in South Africa was not the work of the master hand but the vague, inept effort of Carnarvon, an untrusted subordinate. Disraeli added Cyprus to the Empire, not very reputably. This charming island, to which we have less moral right than to almost any other colony, has been consistently neglected by every British Government from Disraeli's day to ours.

Nevertheless public opinion was coming round. The Queen's Jubilee in 1887 was a festival of Empire stimulated by the appearance of some colonial statesmen in London for informal discussions. Lord Salisbury made motions towards a customs union and a common plan of defence. The dream of a Federal Union of the whole Empire, a fancy that had drifted through men's minds at least since the days of Adam Smith, seemed for a moment near realization. But when Salisbury challenged the Imperial Federation League to draft a constitution they disagreed and dissolved their organization.

What no English statesman appreciated and what the imperialists overlooked was the rise of colonial nationalism. When Kipling wrote of Canada ('Our Lady of the Snows') that she was 'daughter in her mother's house but mistress in her own' he meant well but did not go far enough. The thoughtless use of the term 'mother country' implied a filial subordination which even then no longer existed. Though family ties were strong and the sense of common origins vivid the relation was felt to be on a level of equality—cousinry, shall we say—and cordiality between cousins needs more discreet management than between relatives in the first degree. Canada, as yet the only Dominion, was beginning to claim all the privileges of status which were not assured to her until thirty years later. Already, in the 'nineties, she communicated with the Cabinet through a High Commissioner in London, negotiated her own commercial treaties, and took a line of her own about imperial defence.

Macdonald had won an election in 1878 by advocating a national economic policy for Canada, of building up secondary industries behind a protective tariff. The dilemma then appeared that any plan for a fiscal union of the Empire must reconcile the interest of the colonial loyalists, who were for high protection, with that of the free-traders who made the majority in England. The Little Englanders redoubled their dislike of the colonial *parvenus* in politics who showed, as Goldwin Smith said, 'a strong propensity to the commercial vice of Protectionism, the natural resort of ignorant cupidity', and, worse still, were inclined 'to plunge into all the excesses of Universal Suffrage'.

In 1896 Macdonald's government was replaced by the Liberals under Laurier who held office for fifteen momentous years. Macdonald had stood for high tariffs and closer imperial ties; Laurier was for lower tariffs and reciprocity with the United States. Neither of them was for submission to England's fiscal system under a Federal Senate at Westminster; nor was any other responsible Canadian. Like Smuts in the next generation, Laurier the *canadien* was truly bilingual, a scholar and a gentleman, fully aware of the advantages of the British connexion, and no less aware of his responsibility to Canada. He coined the striking phrase that the nineteenth century belonged to the United States but the twentieth century to Canada. Aided as he was by a revival in world trade, and by the gold rush to the Klondyke, Laurier peopled the prairies. A million immigrants crossed the frontier from the United States, a million came to Canada from northern Europe, and a million from the British Isles during his term of office. Great numbers of them were settled, under agreements with the railway companies on free sections of land in areas which the railways opened up.

This was the final wave of English agricultural migration when, at last, attracted by Laurier's encouragement and the black soil of Manitoba, the settlers went where they might still be British citizens instead of vanishing into the melting-pot of the United States. The overflowing of the excess of British population ended in 1913, the last and best year of mass migration to the Dominions, and incidentally the first year for which accurate and analysed statistics are available. 165,000 British settlers went to Canada, and 56,000 to Australia and New Zealand, whereas only 80,000 went to the United States or other foreign countries.

Laurier showed true statesmanship in raising a

standard to which the moderate men in the two nations of Canada could adhere. At the beginning of the Boer War he carried the country by taking a reasonable line which the Quebec Separatists stigmatized as pro-British, and the Ontario loyalists as pro-French. There, precisely, lay its strength, and there lay the best interest of the Dominion.

At the other end of the world, colonial nationalism made a surprising appearance in New Zealand, an island community that showed no inclination to be drawn into any scheme of federation with the Australian colonies. During the Maori wars the New Zealanders had fallen into disrepute at Westminster and were by no means the favourite children of the mother country that they afterwards became. After an early period of conservatism New Zealand turned sharply radical in 1891, and has remained so. That erratic empire builder, Sir George Grey, who had first governed New Zealand despotically when it was a Crown Colony, and then constitutionally when it attained Responsible Government, retired there in old age and stood for parliament, with a Chartist programme of universal suffrage and no plural voting. A fervid loyalist, he proposed a plan for federating the whole Empire with a draft constitution that foreshadowed the Covenant of the League of Nations. Each colony or Dominion was to begin by devising its own constitution and electing its own governor, under the benevolent patronage of the Queen. But Grey was too cloudy an idealist and too autocratic a leader to succeed in democratic politics; he soon withdrew leaving a radical imperialist tradition to his successors.

New Zealand accordingly embarked upon a series of experiments in social legislation which were then much more advanced than anything of their kind in other countries. Factory and shipping regulations, Industrial Arbitration, Old-age Pensions, Secularized Education, Closer Settlement of the Land, Licensing Reform by Local Option, State Fire and Life Insurance, the Referendum, the Women's Vote: all these political novelties were tried out at an early date in New Zealand, many of them at the instance of Pember Reeves, a brilliant Fabian. For a short time New Zealand led the van of social progress. In the early years of this century it was a little paradise, a pastoral democracy with no class of idle rich and no class of submerged paupers, as nearly the Utopia of the political philosophers as the world has ever seen. But the rate of progress was not maintained and the slump of 1931 found New Zealand somewhat backward in social legislation.

There were, however, two respects in which New Zealand continued to lead the world. The first was the new science of infant welfare which may almost be described as a New Zealand invention. Through the efforts of Dr Truby King, which the whole world imitated, the infant death-rate in New Zealand reached a low level, never previously known and not yet surpassed in any other country. This will be a factor of growing importance in an age when the birth-rate has fallen so low.

The other outstanding feature in New Zealand's history is the solution of the native problem. The self-respect of the Maori race has recovered from the degradation to which they were reduced in the wars, as a result of generous treatment. Their remaining tribal lands were secured to them by treaty and by legislation, which a special branch of the High Court has interpreted liberally in their favour. And they have full political rights under a system of communal representation in the New Zealand parliament. Their tendency to segregate on their own land has been their salvation as a people but, in general terms, it may be said that there is no colour-bar in New Zealand. The minister for native affairs, a full-blooded Maori, has even acted as Deputy Prime Minister of the Dominion. Fifty years ago they numbered less than one twentieth of the total population and seemed to be dwindling towards extinction. They are now increasing more rapidly than the white New Zealanders.

Loyalty to Queen and Empire, which the Little Englanders described as mere infantilism, was nowhere stronger than in the pure democracy of New Zealand. This was a paradox that Englishmen at home never quite understood, since 'loyalty' suggested to them a train of associations—the Established Church, the Old Nobility, the Landed Interest, the Fighting Services—which were unknown to the younger generation in the colonies, or if known were disliked. To the colonists the Empire was already a partnership of free nations under the Crown.

The two conceptions of 'loyalty' produced a dilemma from which Joseph Chamberlain could never extricate himself. In English politics he was an enigmatic figure, the Birmingham Radical, who was thought by the old Tories to be a dangerous revolutionary, a sort of *jacobin*, and by the strait-laced liberals to be a filibustering, financial jingo. If he had made his pile in Australia, before entering politics at forty; if he had been Lord Mayor of Melbourne, instead of Birmingham, and had campaigned there for municipal ownership of utilities, unlocking the land, protection, a wider suffrage, and old-age pensions; such a programme would have naturally been combined with national pride and a desire to strengthen the bonds of Empire. The 'unauthorized programme', which so alarmed Mr Gladstone, would have been commonplace in the colonies. Yet the Birmingham Radical did not appreciate the force of colonial nationalism.

As a social democrat Chamberlain was the man for the colonies, so Merriman of the Cape declared in 1884. But social democrats in England were all free-traders. Chamberlain's hope of an imperial tariff lay in support from the protectionists, that is the Tories. As the champion of imperial federation he was for strengthening not weakening the Imperial Parliament. He therefore could not accept Gladstone's plan of Home Rule for Ireland. Again his campaign for the maintenance of the Union led him into the Tory camp. But this was not at all to the taste of colonial politicians who stoutly believed that self-government had been a blessing to them and would be a blessing to Ireland. Even Cecil Rhodes subscribed to Parnell's fighting fund. Chamberlain's dream of a federated Empire, with devolution of municipal government 'all round', failed to please the English and Irish electorates and, more signally, failed to attract any one of the

Dominions.* The House of Commons was not disposed to admit Canadian and Australian minorities which might prove as troublesome as the Irish Party nor would any Dominion surrender any part of its hard-won liberty to a super-parliament at Westminster. In opposing Home Rule Chamberlain opposed the colonial nationalists; in opposing Free Trade he opposed the majority of the English electorate. The Tory Imperialists who followed Chamberlain's flag misread the signs of the times at home and in the Dominions. Students of politics used to say, in the 'eighties, that the Empire must 'federate or separate' and, in the course of his political progress, Chamberlain indoctrinated a section of the Tories with this belief. We have seen that the Empire neither federated nor separated, but developed into a moral union, such as Dilke had foreseen in his *Greater Britain* (though it excluded the United States).

The testing time came in the Boer War, of which I do not propose to adjudicate the rights and wrongs. From the point of view of the Boers the issue was simple, whether to fight for national independence and self-sufficiency or to compromise with the great Empire that encircled and infiltrated their two republics. They chose to fight, and displayed a national heroism beside which the effort of the Thirteen American Colonies looks puny. From the British

* Though Imperial Federation was so much discussed the only scheme formally submitted by a responsible statesman was laid before the Imperial Conference of 1911 by Sir Joseph Ward of New Zealand. It was rejected by the other Dominions and would probably have been rejected by the New Zealand electorate.

point of view the issue was so complex that only wilful ignorance can describe it as aggression prompted by monopoly capital. The war was not a struggle between 'haves' and have-nots', for Kruger had physical control of the gold mines and never lacked money. It was not a struggle between Englishmen and South Africans, for many thousands of South African loyalists took arms against the Boers. It was not provoked by Chamberlain, who believed until the last days of peace that Kruger could be persuaded to grant to the English in the Transvaal the same rights that the Dutch enjoyed in Cape Colony. Rhodes may have believed that South Africa could be united by the power of money, but Chamberlain disliked Rhodes and opposed his methods. Chamberlain, as always, was set upon achieving federation by diplomatic means. This entanglement may perhaps be resolved, on Marxian principles, in terms of conscious or unconscious pressure by monopoly capital, but no analysis can make the issue simple.

A conflicting feature is the conduct of the other parts of the Empire, and especially such radical colonies as Queensland, Victoria and New Zealand. Throughout the negotiations they were wholehearted in their support of Chamberlain. Rightly or wrongly they envisaged the cause of the Uitlanders on the Rand as a diggers' revolt against oppression, the battle of the Eureka Stockade (see page 59) on a larger scale, and a very apt cause in which to demonstrate the moral unity of the Empire. They were quite uninfluenced by the fluctuations of the Kaffir market, and cared nothing for Cecil Rhodes. Five years later they joined with the

English Liberals and the Boer Generals in protesting against the introduction of Chinese coolies to the Rand. It was not for dividends drawn from indentured labour that they had fought but for political liberty, the guiding principle of the Empire as they understood it.

Canada, the capitalist Dominion, took a less active part in the Boer War. Since Laurier was not confident that he could carry the French-Canadians with him, he contented himself with pronouncing his approval of Chamberlain's policy. Later, under pressure from British-Canadian loyalists, he authorized the despatch of volunteers.

Chamberlain's supposed responsibility for the Boer War drew upon him ferocious personal attacks from the Little Englanders who gloated indecently over British losses in battle. This uproar distracted attention from his work for the colonial territories where his eye foresaw, and his hand left its mark upon, a new world in the tropics. He began by making a revolution in the Colonial Office; that dreary department, wavering between mere despondency and benevolent meddling, was suddenly reorganized on business principles. The new Secretary of State began by installing in his own room a huge terrestrial globe and the electric light. The colonies, he announced, were neglected estates which were to be developed, brought up to date. They must have roads, railways and telegraphs, and public services for health, education and agricultural improvement; all of which cost money. Fifty years earlier, when the War Office and the Colonial Office were combined, angry colonials used to describe their ruler as the Secretary at War with the Colonies. Chamberlain as Colonial Secretary went to war on their behalf against a Chancellor of the Exchequer who stoutly resisted his demands. Of all the countries in the world perhaps New Zealand alone was then willing to spend relatively large sums on constructive national development. The Empire had to wait until 1940 for the establishment of the Colonial Welfare and Development Fund, when Joseph Chamberlain's son was Prime Minister.

There was no way in which these colonies could be developed, in the 'eighties and 'nineties, except by the investment of private capital; and the age produced its characteristic type of *entrepreneur*. The distinction between such men as the Baring brothers, who provided money in the city, and Brassey, who transmuted it into permanent way and rolling stock in the colonies, is relevant in all discussions about 'financial exploitation'. The greatest of the *entrepreneurs* was Cecil Rhodes who used the wealth won at the diamondfields to advance the British frontier to the Zambesi and would have built the Cape-to-Cairo Railway if time had been on his side. A common fault of critics is to speak of Rhodes as though he had been a merchant banker, a man concerned with manipulating money. He was a pioneer, a maker; a man of the open air thinking in terms of land and labour; a man whose mind was set on problems of communications, transport and negotiations with African chiefs; a man who rightly saw that money was the first requisite and luckily had the knack of acquiring it. He must be judged as a frontiersman not as a financier.

CAPITALIST EMPIRE-BUILDERS 99

The great expansion of the nineteenth century was made by men of this type, masterful men who could organize work and handle money, men who were not squeamish and who might easily lapse into what the Americans called filibustering. Some of the smaller fry were mere predatory scoundrels; some were just what is called 'tough'; but the best among them, men like Sir John Forrest in western Australia or Sir George Goldie in Nigeria, were above suspicion of dishonesty. Strathcona's work at Winnipeg was almost on the scale of Rhodes'. The unhappy tale of the Reid concessions in Newfoundland is a similar story with an unhappy ending. It is again to the antipodes that we must look for progressiveness in political economy. Of all these pioneering capitalists Forrest is the one who most intelligently applied the wealth of new found mines to social development. Western Australia is the only one of the southern colonies to be floated into modernity by a financier of this sort.

The original habitat of the species was in North America, where the opening of the West presented on a wider stage the same drama that Rhodes performed in Africa. Much as he admired Oxford culture, it took but a small part in the shaping of his character. His forbears and his natural equals were to be found among the American railway magnates who extirpated the buffalo and the Indian and dreamed dreams 'of far horizons where the strange roads go down'. Even the Jameson Raid is a little garish and unexpected in British history where it has few if any parallels. It is the method by which (when successfully applied) the Americans got possession of California and Texas.

Chamberlain was the first Colonial Secretary to direct towards social progress the potential wealth which the capitalists were beginning to exploit. The activities which had been left to the missionaries were largely taken over as the responsibility of the Colonial Civil Service. But improved communications came first. The building of the Uganda Railway, at the expense of the British taxpayer, the facilities given to Rhodes for a railway to Rhodesia while the rights of the natives were scrupulously guarded, the beginnings of railway construction in Nigeria after the administrative powers of the Royal Niger Company had been taken over; all these brought into existence a new Colonial Empire in Africa for which the method of Indirect Rule was instituted.*

More far-reaching was the effect of founding the West Indian Department of Agriculture and the Schools of Tropical Medicine at Liverpool and London. Popular history, which must dramatize a gradual process, has done well to fix upon that night in August 1897 when Ronald Ross of the Indian Medical Service closed the last link in the chain of researches, planned by Patrick Manson at Liverpool, into the cycle of malarial infection. In the words of the Duke of Windsor, he made one quarter of the world habitable for white men. To take a simple example, the completion of the Panama Canal was made possible

---

* Mention should also be made, though it falls outside this line of argument, of the administrative reforms imposed upon South Africa, after the Boer War, by Chamberlain and Milner. The creation of an efficient public service, much as the Boers hated it at first, was an essential preliminary to the Union.

by mosquito control, according to the principles of Ross and Manson.

For a brief period, with its climax at the Queen's Diamond Jubilee, enthusiasm for the Empire was fashionable in England, even among literary people. Perhaps the two most striking achievements of the English nation are English commercial expansion and English lyric poetry, two lines of activity that, surprisingly, met when the devotees of expansion, efficiency and 'service', found a voice in Rudyard Kipling. After being overrated by contemporaries who read little but him and his imitators, and underrated by a generation of critics who condemned him unread, the bard of Empire has been established at a modest elevation on Parnassus by the measured approval of Mr T. S. Eliot.

Kipling was the poet of the middle-class empire-builders. He showed but small interest in the mass migration of the proletariat and not much more in the condescending patronage of aristocrats and millionaires who saw the world through the windows of first-class carriages. The globe-trotters, the arm-chair philanthropists, the governors born in the purple aroused in him the same scorn as did the remittance men, the parasites of the capitalist system. He drew a distinction between the 'Sons of Mary' who enjoyed the favours of a wealthy society and the 'Sons of Martha' who asked for nothing more than to be cumbered with serving humanity. He described the life of subalterns, district officers, engineers with an aptness of phrase and a power of accurate observation that seemed almost uncanny. For a whole generation of young men, and especially of young men not addicted to aesthetics, Kipling's verses gave life a new direction. Home-sickness was reversed and cockneys yearned for the hardships of life outside Europe, 'fawned on the younger nations—the men that could shoot and ride', and felt an obligation to 'take up the White Man's Burden'.

The critics were quite wrong in supposing that Kipling was complacent about the Empire, or that he preached complacency. The author of 'Recessional' cannot justly be charged with that. He was, however, as indiscreet and perverse about English politics as he was triumphantly right about the smells and sounds and colours of Africa and India. His venomous attacks upon all varieties of English Liberalism, even upon the Liberal Imperialists* who solved the South African problem with bold magnanimity, marked him down for destruction when the fashion in political thinking changed.

Though the Liberal Imperialists directed the overseas policy of Asquith's government (1908–16) the radical Little Englanders prevailed in what are called intellectual circles. Kipling was tabooed by the literary, but continued to provide reading matter and guidance for the subalterns, district officers and engineers who knew nothing of intellectual fashions in London.

* It should be remembered that Chamberlain, Rhodes and Milner were all Liberals by party alignment. Kipling overlooked that.

Chapter VII

ANTI-IMPERIALISM

The reaction produced a change in the meaning of the word 'imperialist', a word with a curious history. Before the eighteen-sixties it meant nothing more than 'the adherent of an emperor'. Sir George Trevelyan used it in 1864, in a book* on British India, to describe a French supporter of Louis Napoleon, with no hint that the word had any special significance in contemporary England. A few years later, in 1878, Lord Carnarvon wrote suspiciously from the Colonial Office asking the meaning of the word 'imperialism' which he was beginning to hear in conversation. That was perhaps judicial ignorance. By the eighteen-eighties the word was in general use to connote the beliefs of a political sect in the value of colonies, the necessity for their closer union, and the need to extend the Empire 'where trade requires the protection of the flag'.†

For thirty or forty years the name of Imperialist was admitted by most respectable Britons, excepting the Little England faction. Blatant imperialism, like blatant patriotism, was eschewed as un-English but, when challenged outright, they would confess to being imperialists in some degree much as they would confess to being patriots.

Gradually the overtones of the word began to acquire a sinister note. The doctrines of imperialism

* *The Competition-wallah.* † *Concise Oxford Dictionary.*

lost credit and the name lost its good repute. Between the German wars it became necessary, in 'advanced' circles, to apologize for being an imperialist. It is only in the last few years that Marxian propaganda has reduced the word to a simple term of abuse. Like 'fascist' or 'bolshevist' the word no longer has any content of meaning when used in political controversy. Both Russians and Americans, in their anti-British moods, make it cover any aspect of British policy which they may happen to dislike: a choice derangement of epithets when, by the dictionary definition, British imperialism is everywhere in retreat; when Russia is consolidating her hold over regions Peter the Great never coveted; when America, in the words of Henry Wallace, is making efforts 'to secure air bases spread over half the globe from which the other half of the globe can be bombed'.*

The case for the opposition was put, in 1903, by J. A. Hobson whose closely reasoned and documented book, *Imperialism*, provided ammunition for the Little Englanders.† Justice will be done to Hobson by quoting here from the summary which he prefixed to the latest edition of his book:

'Whereas various real and powerful motives of pride, prestige, and pugnacity, together with the more altruistic professions of a civilising mission, figured as causes of imperial expansion, the dominant directing motive was the demand for markets and for profitable

* Letter to President Truman, 23 July, 1946.
† The theme is commonplace in the writings of Marx and his followers, but reached the English reading public through Hobson.

investment by the exporting and financial classes within each imperialist regime. The most potent drive towards enlarged export trade was the excess of capitalist production over the demands of the home market. In other words there has been over-saving and underspending. Our concern here is with the urgent drive this situation impels towards the acquisition of foreign markets and areas of lucrative overseas investment.

'The motor-power of Imperialism is not chiefly financial; finance is rather the governor of the imperial engine, directing its energy and determining its work: it does not constitute the fuel of the engine, nor does it directly generate the power. Finance manipulates the patriotic forces which politicians, soldiers, philanthropists, and traders generate; the enthusiasm for expansion which issues from those sources, though strong and genuine, is irregular and blind; the financial interest has those qualities of concentration and clear-sighted calculation which are needed to set Imperialism at work.'

If there is any economic determinism in history it may be admitted that British expansion in the nineteenth century is an example of it. Great Britain had all the factors necessary for imperialism: 'we had the ships, we had the men, we had the money too'. Furthermore, we had the seafaring tradition, the national self-confidence, and the mechanical skill that were equally required; and no other nation had all these material or moral assets. If British expansion in some form or another was economically inevitable, the question remains whether Hobson's explanation of the directing motive is sufficient.

He seemed to disarm his critics by concentrating the argument upon colonial expansion during the 'eighties and 'nineties,* a phase which in his opinion was a reversion to type. The revival of the principle of empire building by means of Chartered Companies with interests both in politics and trade recalled to him the bad old method of the East India Company. It would, he alleged, antagonize the white dominions and lead to the (very desirable) disintegration of the Commonwealth. But development by Chartered Companies proved to be a passing phase; in every instance except British North Borneo, which still (1946) retains its old regime, the political rights of the Chartered Companies were resumed by the Colonial Office, for a consideration.

As in the seventeenth century this form of investment proved disappointing to the shareholders, and the companies showed better profits when relieved of their political responsibilities. Cromer gave a lead in denouncing the concentration of commercial and political power in the same hands, with the result that British imperialism in Egypt and the Sudan has been tolerably free of the taint of the direct profit-motive. But when Chartered Companies were reduced to the status of mere trading companies the anti-imperialists could not find much improvement. The Royal Niger Company brought peace and civilization to an immense

* 1874–88, Federated Malay States, North Borneo, Sarawak; 1884, Papua, Somaliland; 1885, Bechuanaland; 1889, Rhodesia; 1890, Uganda, Kenya, Zanzibar; 1891, Nyasaland; 1893–1900, Solomons, Gilbert and Ellice Islands, Tonga; 1894, final annexation of Kaffraria; 1898, the Sudan; 1900, northern Nigeria.

and potentially wealthy tract of forest and savannah, racked previously by tribal war and by that depraved form of the slave trade which existed to provide victims for human sacrifice. When Lugard organized the colony and protectorate of Nigeria as the shining example of British administration, largely under indirect rule, the function of monopoly-capital was outside his scope. The real progress, which all humane men admire in this backward land during the last fifty years, was progress in things which the last generation valued, and this generation undervalues: internal peace, personal liberty, the rule of law, the suppression of barbarous customs. It was the task of the reformed Colonial Office to separate all this from commercial development. The Royal Niger Company reappeared in the form of the United Africa Company with something like a monopoly in buying produce for export and in distributing imports from Great Britain. Unconsciously and unwillingly the Colonial Office may have been the instrument of monopoly-capital; consciously and willingly it took some pains to draw apart from the connexion.

The problem of Africa in the nineteenth century was anarchy; in the twentieth century it is poverty. How can the standard of life of the African be raised sufficiently to enable him to equip himself with modern social services except by the help of external capital, and how can he get this financial help without enslaving himself to a new master? After wages and interest have been paid who is to enjoy the surplus value of his labour?

Hobson took pains to demonstrate the falsity of the

arguments put forward by imperialists in favour of colonial expansion, and did explode the theory that 'trade follows the flag'. He left unsolved the further problem whether trade ought to follow the flag. Are we not morally obliged to develop a beneficial trade with those countries for which we have assumed political responsibility? After this interval of time Hobson's arguments seem remarkable for their narrow outlook. He builds up a case against one phase of imperialism in a single generation, in order to condemn ten generations of effort in a great variety of circumstances.

There was something prim and acidulous about the Little Englanders; they were too ready to impute base motives. Not only did they accuse Chamberlain of fomenting the Boer War for the benefit of 'the nails and sarsepan business what 'e got 'is money by', but they expected the world to believe that Livingstone and Gordon were the puppets of finance, and that the British built the Aswan Dam in order to plunge the Egyptians into debt.

The pressure of surplus capital seeking an outlet may explain much, but cannot explain the history of the Empire in the days before 1815 when there was no surplus; nor the settlement of the Dominions which, one and all, were hampered in their early days for lack of capital; nor the fact that altruistic empire-builders like Livingstone usually preceded the traders; nor have his arguments much force in an age when the Empire, financially, commercially and politically, has moved into a new set of circumstances. The *gravamen* of Hobson's charge was the financial enslavement of

India, and it is answered by the fact that British exploitation has enabled India to change itself from a debtor to a creditor country.

Yet the current cant about the wickedness* of 'British Imperialism' is still based on Hobson's well-worn arguments, and on not much else. The proper answer was given by Burke when he said that a Great Empire and Little Minds go ill together.

* It should be noted that the British Empire, unlike all other empires past and present, was, in the days of its greatest strength, a Free Trade area, with an Open Door to the commerce of all nations.

Chapter VIII

IMPERIALISM IN RETREAT

The British Empire would not have endured so long had it not been for a discreet sense of moderation in its rulers, generation after generation. The coolness displayed towards the colonies by successive British Governments has at least prevented the empire-builders from overreaching themselves. Some readers may be surprised to learn how many glittering prizes have been let slip by British statesmen who did not seek territorial gains. 'The City' came near to rebellion against King George III for restoring so many conquered colonies to Spain and France at the conclusion of the Seven Years' War: Cuba and the Philippines; Guadaloupe and Martinique; the 'French Shore' of Newfoundland and the site of what is now the Port of Dakar. It showed great prudence on his part not to exact too great concessions from a beaten enemy.

After the fall of Napoleon, when all the colonies of the European states were at England's disposal, we contented ourselves with securing some West Indian and South American plantations where there was already a British element among the settlers, and a few strategic sea-ports. The disposition of the Dutch colonies in 1814 has been much misunderstood. At the request of the Prince of Orange British troops had occupied all the Dutch colonies, after petty fighting in some instances against Quisling officials whom the French had established there in defiance of his authority.

Castlereagh's main object was to create a strong kingdom of the Netherlands under the House of Orange and he restored to it the prize of the Dutch Empire, Java, the richest island in the world. Britain retained Cape Town and the Ceylonese sea-ports, which Dutch and British alike regarded as strategic not commercial possessions, paying for them a sum in compensation, which the Dutch Government gratefully, enthusiastically, accepted, a diplomatic transaction hardly influenced by commercial considerations. So little did Castlereagh care for colonial expansion that his enemies accused him of re-ceding Java because he couldn't find it on the map.

At one time or another in the course of European wars, British armies have occupied almost every* island in the Mediterranean. In many instances they appeared as liberators or protectors; remained at the entreaty of the inhabitants; attempted—with little success—to introduce British political liberties; and withdrew when their mission was accomplished. Thus Corsica was once a self-governing Dominion of the Crown, Sicily a protectorate with a constitution based on that of Great Britain, the Ionian Islands a federal republic under a British High Commissioner. Luckily for the liberty of Europe the British régime in Malta was less short-lived.

Between the years 1876 and 1936 the British made similar interventions, on a larger scale, throughout the Arab world. The beginnings of this phase of expansion go back a hundred years to the days when

* All the larger islands, except Sardinia, and many of the smaller islands.

the Bombay Government was establishing sea-power in the Arabian Sea. In 1839 Aden was occupied and, even earlier, treaty relations were formed with the Sultanates of southern Arabia. Next the coming of the steamship led to an agitation for quicker mail services to India, and thus to the Overland Route through Egypt. Anglo-French rivalry took the form during the 'sixties of a struggle for spheres of influence in the Levant which the French regarded as a field for political domination and the British as a channel for trade with India. The British favoured railway communications and at first derided the French fancies about a canal through the Isthmus of Suez. With every inducement from foreign financiers, and a spendthrift disposition, the Khedive Ismail was very pleasantly hurried along the road to ruin.

After Sedan the French were obliged to cut their losses and could not prevent Disraeli from buying the bankrupt Khedive's shares in the Suez Canal which they had insisted on constructing. They also refused to support Gladstone when he sent the fleet to uphold the legitimate Egyptian Government against a murderous revolt. Though Gladstone assured himself that he was protecting the Khedive from the consequences of his own folly, and was doing so by virtue of international agreements, he could not avoid the imputation of imperialism. He sent an army of occupation to Egypt and it has stayed there for two whole generations. Until 1898 the war in the Sudan justified the occupation; it is perhaps regrettable that the Liberals, in their long tenure of office before 1914, neither withdrew the troops from the Delta nor regulated their status.

THE PARTITION OF THE TURKISH EMPIRE

Among the by-products of the first German war was the destruction of the Turkish Empire by Britain and her Dominions. That would have been a surprise to Dilke and Froude, if they had lived to see it. A partition of Turkey in Asia, by the joint effort of Britain, France and Russia had long been a possibility, but that Britain should have been allowed to complete the task almost alone was quite unexpected.

The Armistice of 1918 found the British Empire at the zenith of its powers: impoverished but still dominant in the trade and finance of the world; exhausted but protected by a Navy, an Army and an Air Force that none could excel; unfederated but possessed of wider territory than ever before. And the three campaigns, in the Dardanelles, Palestine and Mesopotamia, had given the British a commanding position throughout Islam. From Khartoum to Singapore the whole Moslem world lay within the British sphere of influence, while Russia on the northern flank was too distraught to constitute a serious rival.

Surely there must be some secret affinity between Englishmen and Arabs. Does the Puritan strain in the strongest English natures find something akin to itself in the character of the Bedouin who are at once passionate Moslems and passionate egotists? English literature, especially, is rich in tales of solitary adventures among these desert dwellers whose stark way of life is the opposite extreme to soft English comfort. From the haughty Kinglake and the eccentric Hester Stanhope through the bold, rakish Richard Burton and the mild 'nazarene physician', Charles Doughty, there is a succession, almost a dynasty, of Arabian travellers, all remarkable for their courage, their style, and their pronounced individuality. Gordon and Kitchener knew the fascination of the desert; and for those now middle-aged it is best expressed by T. E. Lawrence, though he is by no means the last of the line. Throughout the Arab area the influence of Great Britain has been exercised by the force of character of solitary individuals such as these, men who feel an instinctive sympathy with the Arabs. They occur frequently in the British Race and are rare in other nations.

Since T. E. Lawrence has now receded into that period of history about which most citizens know least, the generation before their own, it may be useful to recall the circumstances of his brief fame. He was one of a band of British soldiers sent to organize a revolt of the desert Arabs against the Turks. Being expert in the affairs of Syria and Palestine, he planned to carry the revolt out of the desert into the settled provinces, giving it the character of a national rising of citizens and peasants as well as of Bedouin. He selected, and imposed upon his colleagues, the Prince who was to be the national leader, whose family now rules in Irak and Transjordania. Lawrence had no illusions about the scale of his campaigns in relation to Allenby's great battles. He did, however, show his flag in Damascus; set up an Arab Government there, and withdrew.

There ensued a period of confusion caused by rivalry between the British and the French, and by a deplorable duplicity in British policy. The High Commissioner in Egypt had promised that the British would liberate Arabia, Syria, and Mesopotamia with reservations covering the Syrian Coast, where the population was mixed, and some unspecified areas where the French might assert their rights. But, simultaneously, the Foreign Office, perhaps through inadvertence, made a secret treaty with France dividing the whole Arab area into French and British 'zones of influence'. At the end of the war the French repudiated the whole of Lawrence's arrangements and insisted upon occupying their zone which included Damascus. It was this betrayal that embittered Lawrence's later years. Nevertheless a slight improvement came when the zones of influence were converted into mandates under the League of Nations. His dream of Empire had been a group of self-governing oriental states freely associated with Great Britain, as were the white Dominions, and bound to her by ties of honour and gratitude.

In 1921 Lloyd George transferred the negotiation from the Foreign Office to the Colonial Office, that is from Lord Curzon to Mr Churchill, who persuaded Lawrence to join his staff. The Middle East Settlement of 1922 should be regarded as one of Mr Churchill's greatest achievements; it even satisfied Lawrence who prophesied, accurately, that it would stand for fifteen years. The two new Arab kingdoms were created under mandate, and at the same time the first steps were taken towards the independence of Egypt. The progressive release of these three countries from British control is the only example of such a procedure in the history of empires, for which due credit should be taken, and given. Best of all it was a vindication of

British honour, by which the friendship of Englishmen and Arabs has been preserved.

Fifteen years after the Settlement the Levant was again plunged into disorder by events in Palestine. That unhappy district had been reserved in the original pledge given to the Arabs, and was offered to the Zionists as the site of a 'Jewish National Home' by Lord Balfour, in 1917. In the pride of our power we accepted the mandate for this thankless task which the Americans declined. There was no profit or advantage in it, and little prospect of gratitude. This was the last forward step of British imperialism, and a harsh warning against quixotry in politics. It was inevitably a cause of offence to our friends the Arabs. It earned us no thanks from the Jewish colonists* who found the country too limited for their ambitions. The poor Jews of Central Europe blamed the British because the Promised Land could not receive them all; the rich Jews of America, deeply conscious of their own guilt in neglecting their persecuted brethren, chose the British as the scapegoat of their own sins.

'To propose that Great Britain should voluntarily give up all authority over her colonies was to propose such a measure as never was and never will be adopted by any nation in the world': so wrote Adam Smith during the American War. Yet the history of the British Empire has now for many years recorded example after example of prudent withdrawals and discreet surrenders of sovereignty, a policy which whist-players call discarding from strength. The

* Yet the Jewish National Home is a more perfect example of systematic colonization than any in British colonial history.

highest point in the curve of British Imperialism, which I should place in the year 1921, was the moment when our material strength was greatest and the tendency to discard from strength most apparent. Much later we find British statesmen, as if they were still the opulent masters of the world, light-heartedly abandoning legitimate rights and interests, as in Egypt and the Sudan, while retaining unprofitable and unhonoured duties, as in Palestine.

For a hundred years Britannia had ruled the waves of every ocean and sea almost unchallenged. In the First German War she had met a challenge and had emerged from the contest victorious, still the first naval power in the world, but now only first among potential equals. Her wise abdication from the empire of the sea by the Naval Limitations Treaty signed at Washington in 1922 was prompted by the Dominions whose statesmen gave warning that the Anglo-Japanese alliance would not stand fire. The struggle for power in the Pacific as it was then foreseen must be conceived in terms of spheres of influence. Better to compromise and withdraw than to bluster and be defeated.

From that moment Hong Kong, which British law and administration had made into the greatest free port in the world, was indefensible. The British strategy, designed to protect sea-trade by sea-power, was based upon a line of vital points: Gibraltar, Malta, Suez, Aden, Colombo, Singapore, the last essential to the defence of Australasia; but Hong Kong was left 'out on a limb'. No more need be said of the lamentable story of Singapore save that some efforts were made to fortify it in spite of obstruction by the Labour Party. It fell, in 1942, because the weakness of our Air Forces obliged us to concentrate them west of Suez.

It was the negotiation over Naval Disarmament in 1921 that first made clear to American observers the hidden strength of the world-wide British commerce. Its nervous system was the network of submarine cables which were, in many regions of the world, a British monopoly and half the secret of sea-power. The Royal Navy in the 1914 war had cut all German overseas communications, had kept all British communications at work, had controlled all cable traffic, and had laid many strategic lines. Remote British dependencies—Fanning Island, the Cocos Islands, Ascension—were found to have a new significance.

In British administrative circles there had long been an obscure struggle between the advocates of public and private ownership of the cable services. The Colonial Office and the Pacific Dominions were inclined towards the former, the Treasury and the Post Office towards the latter course. One of Chamberlain's triumphs had been to drive the Treasury into an agreement to finance the 'All-Red' cable across the Pacific under the joint management of the United Kingdom, Canada, Australia and New Zealand. After the First German War the 'All-Red Route' was for a time extended round the world by the purchase of rights over other systems. Pressure from the commercial telegraph companies, who were beginning to suffer from American competition, led to a reversal of policy in 1929. All the principal lines and services, whether publicly or privately owned, were merged into the corporation now known as Cables and Wireless Ltd., with representatives of the British Government on the Board.

Whatever may be thought of a reversion to commercial ownership, it must be admitted that a unified service enabled the British to dominate the field of propaganda in the Second German War. A site could be found on British soil for a terminal from which any part of the world could be reached by submarine cable or by radio. The new American imperialism attempts to place itself on an equal footing by occupying rival sites.

Whereas the British system was designed to cover British sea-borne trade along the old routes, the American plan for a new world strategy is based on the assumptions that men and mails will travel by air, following 'great circles' across the Arctic regions, and that 'point-to-point' radio networks will supersede the old submarine cables. It is not to be supposed that the Suez Canal will be deserted like the green waterways of Old England, or that heavy goods will travel by air; but priority traffic, taking new short cuts, will no longer be dependent upon British goodwill.

The retreat from imperialism is most marked in the case of British India, the largest of our acquisitions and the one in which our position is hardest to define. The simple explanation is often given that we went there first for trade and stay there primarily for the sake of the export market. But in the days of John Company we never found a staple there either for export or import. It was only after the assumption of authority by the Crown that India began to import British manufactures and British capital in great amounts. In 1938, the last year of peaceful trade, about one-twelfth of British exports, in value, were absorbed by India's 450 million inhabitants, at the average rate of one and elevenpence per head. Argentina, outside the Empire, though its population is only one-twentieth of India's population, took more than half that gross amount at the average rate of thirty shillings per head. It does not appear upon the face of it that India's trade is necessary to our survival or that it need decline if India becomes independent and prosperous.

Was it sheer lust for glory that directed the British conquest? Certainly not in the days of the Company when the proprietors repeatedly censured aggressive governors. Hardly more so under the Crown, though it would be difficult to acquit some British administrations of playing at power politics in central Asia and using the Indian army for other ends than India's security. Yet, taking the longer view, the Indian army has not been unduly bloated. At all times, including the present, it has been very much smaller than the Russian army though raised for the defence of a very much larger population.

When James Mill uttered the sneer that the Empire existed to provide 'outdoor relief for the Upper Classes' his words contained the grain of truth that is often found in bitter epigrams. The strength of the British connexion has been the export of educated Englishmen to the Indian services. Authority, a habit that grows with use, is not willingly resigned. Those families which have a long association with India form an aristocracy that has no peers in history, and that will not be shamed out of its self-respect by a little reactionary ingratitude. Responsibility and hard work were what they sought and what they found in India. So far from amassing riches were they that few even achieved fullness of days. In the old times a minority of the fresh-faced lads who set out from Haileybury and Addiscombe survived to enjoy their pensions at Bath or Cheltenham. They loved India and often died for it, even though India loved them not.

Whatever the motive, they created in India such national unity as it possesses, giving it an army, a judiciary, a civil service, a penal code, a public works department, a system of famine relief, roads, railways and telegraphs, irrigation works on the largest scale, and—most important of all—a common language. Macaulay's Minute on Education which led to the adoption of the English language as the medium and English culture as the substance of instruction remains, what Seeley declared it to be, the outstanding event of British rule in India. The National Congress itself, founded under English auspices, debates in English according to the rules of English parliamentary procedure. In the end the hardest responsibility of all was laid upon the faithful English servants of India, the duty to resign. There is more nobility in that than in anything that has gone before.

Men of vision among the British rulers of India have always foreseen the coming of a time when Indians would be raised to self-government by British efforts. Macaulay spoke to that effect in the House of Commons in 1833. During the crisis of the Mutiny Henry

Lawrence declared his faith in India's future freedom, and the Queen's proclamation of 1858, by abolishing all distinction of caste or creed in the public service, seemed to bring the day a little nearer. But the Mutiny had been a sore setback; it tended to convince the British that the day was still far distant.

Seventy or eighty years ago most observers of the Empire assumed that the white Dominions were on the point of final separation whereas British India would stand for generations. The early Free-Traders assumed that the perversely protectionist colonies did not deserve to belong to the Empire but that India, luckily, could be forced to accept the blessings of Free Trade. Seeley's sardonic criticism* of British rule was concluded with the telling phrase that 'a time may conceivably come when it may be practicable to leave India to herself, but for the present it is necessary to govern her as if we were to govern her for ever'. It was an obligation of honour to complete our task in Asia.

Recent Indian history does not make edifying reading. If it were true that sabotage and non-co-operation had forced the hands of the British the outlook would be black indeed, for a government of free men by free men is not achieved in this way. If we are to entertain a hope for India's liberty and honour it will be better to suppose that something is due to the patient and gradual process by which the British have introduced natives of India into all posts of authority, and have built up elective institutions from below, in the face of much obstruction and abuse.

* *The Expansion of England*, 1883.

Chapter IX

DOMINION STATUS

Devolution of authority which may be considered a weakening of British might in Asia has without doubt increased the strength of the 'white' Commonwealth. Virtual independence under the name of Dominion Status has brought the Dominions into a more genuine and effective partnership with the mother country than was ever achieved in the days when the formal sovereignty of Parliament was asserted. It was a dangerous legal fiction that might please constitutional lawyers but contained the seeds of political trouble. The history of the bill which was enacted in November 1931 under the bombastic title of the Statute of Westminster is complex and somewhat puzzling.

In theory and in practice Dominion Status had been understood and approved by all parties for twelve years before the Statute was drafted. After fighting as belligerent nations in the First German War the Dominions were parties to the Treaty of Versailles and original members of the League of Nations. Final recognition of their status may be ascribed to the day in 1926 when M. Raoul Dandurand of Canada presided over the Assembly which then elected Canada to a vacancy on the Council of the League.

Meanwhile agreement had been reached tacitly at several Imperial Conferences not to formulate the precise meaning of Dominion Status, since definition limits growth. While this was the policy of the loyalists, it was the separatist, Hertzog of South Africa, austerely trained in the Roman-Dutch law, who insisted upon a definition at the Conference of 1926. He claimed to have originated the operative phrase in the Balfour Declaration, 'autonomous communities freely associated as members of the British Commonwealth'; and returned to announce to his supporters in South Africa that 'the old British Empire is no more'. The process that to his narrow logical mind seemed to be disintegration appeared in a different light to his rival Smuts, the philosopher of 'Holism', as synthesis, the creation of a higher unity by the removal of obstructive limitations. Hertzog spent the remainder of his public life in restless assertions of national rights. He would not be content with 'free association' but must always be probing to make sure that no concealed restrictions survived, 'like a bridegroom (as Botha said of him many years earlier) who spends the honeymoon considering what to do if the bride should prove unfaithful'.

After the Balfour Declaration the loyalists would have been glad to let constitutional theory alone. The impulse to implement the Declaration by legal enactment arose from questions about the competence of South African and Canadian courts in certain lawsuits. Statutory definition was provided by a conference of learned lawyers.

No schoolboy in the Dominions will ever be required to memorize and recite the Statute of Westminster as American boys memorize the Declaration of 4 July, or as Roman boys memorized the Law of

BACKGROUND TO STATUTE OF WESTMINSTER 125

Twelve Tables. It declares no new principle of political philosophy and contains no rhetoric, but briefly, in technical language, makes certain amendments in the Colonial Laws Validity Act, 1865. It may be safely asserted that no one in 1931 other than constitutional lawyers had ever heard of this Act which was not mentioned in any standard political history; it defined the power of the Crown to disallow acts of Colonial legislatures in case of repugnancy with the laws of England; and had been a dead letter for forty years, except when colonial courts had made a convenience of it. The obsolescent legal principle of repugnancy was not likely to stir the blood of voters in New Zealand or Ontario. The remaining clauses of the Statute of Westminster are mainly reservations and exceptions made by particular Dominions, from a certain doubt where the Statute was leading them.

So far as the lawyers were concerned the Statute served its purpose of straightening out some small discrepancies, particularly in commercial law. In the political field its effects were less propitious. It was proposed in the House of Commons by Mr J. H. Thomas, supported by Sir Stafford Cripps for the Labour Party and Mr Amery for the Conservatives, but was strongly opposed by Mr Churchill on the grounds that it played into the hands of the Irish separatists and thus might provide a dangerous precedent in future negotiations for self-government in India. After a lively debate the Bill was passed by a vote of 350 to 50 on a substantive amendment.

The Statute was received with suspicion by loyalists in the Dominions though, where there was goodwill, it could do no harm. Its inflammable properties might have been expected to appear in the case of the three Dominions where small nationalities were 'encysted' in the British organism: Canada, South Africa, Southern Ireland. The French-Canadians, resting their privileges upon the British North America Act, which is expressly declared to be unaffected by the Statute of Westminster, have made no use of it. A majority of South Africans have, since 1931, given their votes for the generous policy of Smuts against the narrow provincialism of Hertzog and his successors. The Southern Irish have behaved much as Mr Churchill foretold.

Magnanimity, that rare virtue in politics for which Burke vainly pleaded in 1775, has not been wanting in the later history of the Empire and, when displayed at the centre, has often met with a generous response from the provinces. But there are no final solutions to the problems of politics which dissolve only to crystallize in a new form. Constitutions that outlast the lives of their founders are to be accounted longaevous above the average, at least of the twentieth century. The preservation of *canadien* and *afrikaner* societies within the Commonwealth under guarantee from British Acts of Parliament, the one for eighty the other for forty years, is an achievement in which the British may take pride, whatever they may imagine about the future of these nationalities. Those who have faith in the ideal of free government will pay a tribute too to those *canadiens* and *afrikaners* who were bold enough to take up the partnership. Without Laurier and Smuts would Dominion Status have come to maturity?

For a few years after the Irish Treaty there was a hope that General Smuts's example would inspire a reconciliation with the Southern Irish, had not Mr Cosgrave, who might have stood beside Laurier and Smuts in history, been replaced by Mr De Valera, soon after the Statute of Westminster was enacted. Like Hertzog, Mr De Valera chose to use the Statute as a wedge for splitting the nations apart. But 'free association' must be taken at its actual worth; the partners in the Commonwealth are free to go or free to come and, when the deplorable pedantries of Mr De Valera are forgotten, some warmer-hearted Irishman may find a better use for the Statute of Westminster.

Has it indeed been so severe a blow to Great Britain that Mr De Valera withdrew his countenance from us during the second war against German tyranny? It was the first of Britain's wars in which there was not an army of Irish volunteers aiding our enemies against us, the first in which we were not obliged to detach troops to guard against an Irish rebellion. Again the 'wild geese' were fighting

> 'Head to the storm as they faced it before!
> For where there are Irish there's bound to be fighting,'

but in this war the Irish volunteers fought on our side, and gave us our two greatest generals.

Writers on the British Empire have not explored the reactions of Irish history upon the other colonies; for, in the seventeenth century, Ireland was a colony too. The language of colonization with its talk of plantations, settlers and natives was habitually used of

Ireland. The same men using the same methods colonized Virginia and Ulster. Archdeacon Cunningham professed to have found in the foundation of Charleston a direct imitation of the foundation of Derry. Everyone knows that an agitation for Irish independence was simultaneous with the American Revolution but not whether there was contact between the leaders. Were the Scotch-Irish who were so prominent in Washington's campaigns in league with the protestant United Irishmen? Fifty years later the Colonial Reformers gave much thought to Irish poverty and emigration. Was the reluctance of Peel to accede to their demands hardened by a resolution not to grant to Canadian politicians what he dared not grant to Daniel O'Connell? The Irish famine by setting the great Catholic emigration in motion changed the tone and tendency of American politics. Australia received her share of the migrants and felt the same stimulus. The policy of Home Rule for the Colonies but not for Ireland poisoned imperial relations from 1886 to 1921 and, when a plausible solution was found to the Irish problem, it was expressly stated to be a repetition of what had been done in Canada. In Ireland's long and tragic story the intermittent appearances of the Dominions, as they progressed towards partnership with Great Britain, provided a continuous underplot, a hopeful indication since their story has a happy ending.

CHAPTER X

OUTLOOK FOR THE FUTURE

Three times in the last fifty years have Britain's enemies announced with glee that the old tyrant of the seas was down at last. The Boer War and each of the German wars were assumed to be death blows to the British Empire which would disintegrate under the strain. Yet such disintegration as has occurred has been voluntary devolution, and so far it has not detracted from the Empire's strength. We are weakened but not by treachery. It is not necessary to expatiate upon the loss of our overseas investments, as the result of wars, and the consequent decline in our bargaining power, though it may be worth while to recall that our loss has meant financial gain, in some degree, to the Dominions and to India. Far more serious is the sterilizing of our future hopes by the decline in the birth-rate. British strength was in men before it was in money, in the younger sons, of rich and poor families alike, who were not content to mope at home on parental allowances or on poor-relief but sought their fortune where fortunes were to be found. It is now Old England that needs systematic colonization with new men and money.

We sometimes lay claim to a mature sense of political realities which we deny to other nations; we should not be intimidated by the inevitable. Sixty years ago Seeley plainly foretold the approach of a time when Russia and the United States would surpass Great Britain by weight of numbers; and that time has come.

> 'Far-called, our navies melt away;
>   On dune and headland sinks the fire:
> Lo, all our pomp of yesterday
>   Is one with Nineveh and Tyre!'

The tale is threadbare: 'time hath his revolution; there must be a period and an end to all temporal things, *finis rerum*, an end of names and dignities, and whatsoever is terrene'. And why not of the British Empire? It is clear that in the time of anyone now living we can not again resume that care-free proliferation of men and goods that burgeoned in the eighteen-sixties. On the contrary we must husband our resources.

The three concentric rings of British influence will provide a conventional scheme for reviewing the situation. The inner ring, the colonies of settlement now reconstituted as the British Commonwealth, stands firmer than ever before. The increased strength of the junior partners sets off the reduced strength of the senior partner in almost every respect except that of population, for they too exhibit a very low birth-rate. No longer can the Dominions be regarded as a boundless reserve of agricultural land held for the benefit of land-hungry Britons, since that class of persons has almost vanished, both at home and in the Dominions.

Though the whole British Race shows signs of becoming urbanized it would be rash to deduce that this implies degeneration; it is merely the end towards which industrial civilization has been driving for a hundred years. The fancy of some Utopians, that a distributive peasant society might return 'as it was in the Golden World', has been dissipated by machine power and the division of labour, with the result that the workers on settled lands expect the amenities of Cosmopolis, and the frontiersmen tame the wilderness with engines and laboratories. The figure of John Bull, that sturdy stupid yeoman, asking for nothing better than the produce of his own land, is no longer the national type. Mr Bernard Shaw's engineer, Henry Straker,* would make a better model for caricaturists in the twentieth century. With all the old English good sense and good humour, and most of the old English prejudices, he is more a rover even than his father. Luckily, looking back over the last seven years we need have no doubts of his stamina or courage. Above all he has taken to the air as aptly as his ancestors took to the ocean. Nothing is farther from the truth than to describe him as a proletarian. In all the English-speaking countries today the problem is to find hands to do hard manual labour in a society where all are determined to join the *bourgeoisie*. The future of these countries appears to depend upon their success in finding a way of getting these tasks done by labour-saving devices before the breed of coal miners and farm labourers is extinct. Otherwise the choice will lie between conscription, cheap foreign labour and poverty. When Adam refuses to dig, and Eve dictates her own conditions of work in the spinning-mill, where's the proletarian?

Accordingly British migration in the twentieth century has taken the form of a middle-class move-

* 'My business is to do away with labour. You'll get more out of me and a machine than you will out of twenty labourers.' (*Man and Superman.*)

ment, the exchange of technicians, teachers, business executives, scientific workers, professional men and lively youngsters of both sexes, with comparative freedom, between one part of the Empire and another. What matter if the tide flows from London to Sydney or ebbs from Sydney to London provided that the migrants individually and the Commonwealth as a whole benefit from the movement. This circulation between the heart and the extremities maintains the life of the organism, the moral unity that transcends the narrower nationalisms. To be a British subject, with the freedom of this league of nations, is still the greatest political privilege the world can offer.

Between the countries of the Commonwealth and the Colonial Dependencies there is a similar migratory flow of men and women going to make their living by public service or useful commerce. But, in summarizing British relations with this second ring of British influence, it is necessary to distinguish between the backward provinces and the Asiatic civilizations which have been dominated by British 'imperialism'. In the Arab world it would hardly be an exaggeration to say that we appeared as liberators and are withdrawing, having done our work. In India, whether we erred in the past or not, we are now the anxious *accoucheurs* of Indian liberty. It is to be supposed that Ceylon and Burma will follow India's path, though there is no reason why they should deprive themselves of the benefit of entering as free partners into the Commonwealth. Very different is the situation in Malaya and the East Indies. In all this rich and populous region every step that the British took forward, except the last, was with the full concurrence of the inhabitants. The great city of Singapore is a British foundation to which the traders of all nations flocked to enjoy British law and liberty. The rubber-plant which makes Malaya rich was introduced by the British; the tin was found and worked by British enterprise. The system of government, by indirect rule over the greater part of the area, was guaranteed by treaty and based upon the long tradition of the people. To put back the clock by the arbitrary annexations of 1946 was an incomprehensible act. There has been nothing like it in British imperial history since Dalhousie provoked the Indian Mutiny by annexing Oudh; and there was far less justification in Malaya.

The natural wealth and the mixed population of Malaya place it on a different footing from the impoverished or backward colonies in other regions, which may be considered in three groups:

First, the West Indies once so high in public estimation and now, it seems, perpetually depressed. Their legend of a golden age refers to the time of the French wars which gave a scarcity value to their products and brought them naval and military establishments with money to spend. Otherwise, between hurricanes, pestilences and fluctuations in the price of sugar, they have never enjoyed long periods of prosperity. Once they were regarded as a field for white settlement until the African slave trade gave them a population better suited to the climate. If their traditional loyalty at last meets with some return, in the form of capital investment for the benefit primarily of the borrowers, British science, island fertility, and the willingness of the West Indians may yet make British political institutions a blessing to them.

Secondly, there are the primitive territories in Africa which stand to gain most from the Colonial Development and Welfare Fund. The jealousy that once inflamed the breast of England's enemies over these colonies has somewhat subsided; and the abuse hurled at the Colonial Office on their account, by the Little Englanders, is pitched in a lower key. Since Chamberlain diverted the course of the Colonial Office into constructive channels its conduct in East and West Africa has been so patently beneficial to the natives as to disarm enlightened criticism. Black Africa must, however, adjust itself to meet two dangers before it can attain to freedom. The development of its resources may imply the growth of an unbalanced society like that of the West Indies in the past, when cultivators have grown nothing but cash crops for the benefit of investors and mortgagors overseas. It is the duty of the Colonial Office to find means of financing the African without enslaving him to the financier.

The other danger is the undefined frontier of White Man's Country, for Africa is under-populated and can receive many more white settlers in suitable regions. In the Union of South Africa, as in the Southern States of America, certain types of labour are held to be beneath the dignity of a white man. If black men must be called in for unskilled labour in white man's country the line of demarcation vanishes and the demand for black labour depopulates the black man's country. It will be a final shame upon the Colonial Office if it fails to protect black Africa from white exploitation.

Though the Colonial Empire is a trust, and though trusteeship is by nature temporary, the trust should never be relinquished until the natives can protect their own rights. The worst peril is the impatience of the small class of educated natives who demand liberty before they are strong enough to defend it.

The other group includes the forgotten colonies, the miscellaneous islands that once had strategic importance or once supplied some commodity long since superseded. The great island of Newfoundland with its 300,000 British settlers has barely escaped from this category. Having over-capitalized itself in the effort to develop its inland resources the island now seems obliged to fall back upon its staple product, the harvest of the sea. But Newfoundland lies in the centre of the world's new traffic ways, and may again be in the front of the stage. Saint Helena was a vital point in our system of sea-power for 150 years, and may be again. Who would have thought, ten years ago, that the Seychelles and Papua would mean so much to us in war? Mauritius with its French aristocracy and growing population of Indian coolies has a historic past, and may have a future. Though some of the many islands like these have deteriorated in their utility to us they are still valuable to their inhabitants. Those who conceive of Empire in terms of duties rather than of rights should not be content to leave these properties on a basis of 'care and maintenance'.

There remains the outer ring, the British sphere of influence, which no longer expands in harmony with the growth of trade. Hobson's case against British imperialism has quite lost its force at a time when a socialist government is urging the British people to reduce consumption in order to export necessities which we could very well use at home. No doubt the nation of shopkeepers, with its rich old connexion and a world-wide list of customers who have expressed their satisfaction in the past, will recover some substantial fragments of the old commerce. But the goodwill of the business that the British carried round the world was a more lasting asset than their stock-in-trade. The use of the English language meant the propagation of certain principles that are implicit in its vocabulary. The English language spreads more rapidly than before and may in time become, perhaps in some rationalized form, the universal means of communication.

With the language goes the literature; wherever the tongue of Shakespeare is understood a voice will bear witness for individualism, even for eccentricity, for a belief in the efficacy of tolerance and compromise, for a sense of liberty based on common-law rights, above all for the untranslatable spirit of fair-play which is so different from abstract justice. Though it may be thought frivolous to stress these idiosyncrasies they are the outward signs of the English Liberal Protestant tradition, the faith and morals that Milton held, and Britain's best gift to mankind.

Three modes of imperialism, the privilege of membership in the Commonwealth to which the door stands open, advancement of the Colonial Dependencies, and dissemination of the English Ideal offer to the world greater benefits in the coming age than in the past.

INDEX

Aborigines, protection of, 43
Aden, 117
Afghanistan, 71
Africa, Black, 134; South, 7, 14, 77–83, 95–8; West, 18
Afrikaners, 126
'All-Red-Route', 118
America, U.S., 6, 29–33, 35, 63
Appeals, Statute of, 1
Arabia, 112–16
Arthurian legend, 2
Atlantic voyages, 18–20
Australia, 7, 55–9, 60, 99, 128

Bacon, Francis, 19, 21–2
Barbados, 21
Baring Brothers, 64–5
Barker, Sir E., 8
Basutoland, 78
Bermuda, 21
Birthrate, 129–30
Bloemfontein, 78
Boër War, 95
Boers, the, 77–8, 95
Bombay, 17
Botany Bay, 36
Brassey, T., 63
British Crown, influence of, 16
British North America Act, 66–7
British Race, expansion of, 4–5
Buenos Aires, 10, 37
Buller, Charles, 45
Burma, 132

Cable stations, 118–19
Calcutta, 17
Canada, 7; Arctic, 19; Upper, 33; 60, 64–5, 86–90
Canterbury Settlement, 53–4
Cape Coast Castle, 18
Cape Colony, 44
Capital, export of, 61–4
Carnarvon, Lord, 79–80, 103
Castlereagh, Lord, 111
Cawnpore, 74
Ceylon, 132
Chamberlain, J., 81, 93–4, 96–7
Chamberlain, N., 98
China, 13, 29
Churchill, W., 115, 125
Climate and colonization, 5
Cobden, R., 84
Colombo, 117
Colonial Institute, Royal, 85; Office, 45, 82, 84, 97, 107; Reformers, 44, 128; types, 9, 14, 57–8
Columbia, British, 56
Commonwealth, British (the name), 3
Concentric rings of Empire, 4, 130

Dalhousie, Lord, 70, 73
Dandurand, R., 123
Dependencies, Colonial, 132
De Valera, E., 127
Diamond jubilee, 101
Dilke, Sir C., 1, 86
Disraeli, B., 79, 88, 112

INDEX

Dominion status, 123
Durham, Lord, 7, 25, 44-5
Dutch colonies, 110-11

East India Company, 29, 36, 39, 68
East Indies, British, 132
Egypt, 112, 115
Empire, the word, 1-2; First and Second British, 2; strategy, 36; under the Stewarts, 23-4
English language, 11-12, 136
Eureka Stockade, 59
Evangelicals, 40

Federation, Imperial, 88, 94-5
Forrest, Sir J., 99
France, 28, 110
Free Trade, 83-4, 109
French-Canadians, 126
French fleet, 33, 115
Frere, Sir B., 80
Frobisher, M., 19
Froude, J. A., 85-6
Fulton, R., 35

George III, 29-31, 110
Georgia, 24, 31
Gibraltar, 28, 33, 117
Gilbert, Sir H., 19-20
Gladstone, W. E., 45, 85, 112
Gold rushes, 54-6
Goldie, Sir G., 99
Granville, Lord, 85
Grey, Henry Earl, 47, 64
Grey, Sir G., 78, 85, 86, 91

Hakluyt, R., 19
Hertzog, J. B., 124
Hobson, J. A., 104-9

Hong Kong, 17, 117
House of Commons, 125
Hudson's Bay, 28; H.B.C., 64
Hyderabad, 69

Imperialism, 83, 88, 103
India, 13, 30, 38, 68-76, 119, 120-2, 132; governors and viceroys, 38; Indian Mutiny, 68, 73-4; railways, 76
Irak, 114-15
Ireland, 127-8
Irish emigrants, 49-51
Islam, 113

James II, 24-5
Jameson Raid, 81, 99

Kabul, 71
Khyber Pass, 70
Kimberley, 79
King, Dr Truby, 92
Kipling, R., 72, 101-2
Klondyke, 56
Kruger, Paul, 81

Latin America, 37
Laurier, Sir W., 89-90, 97
Lawrence, John, 72, 76
Lawrence, T. E., 114-15
League of Nations, 123
Leeward Islands, 21
Liberals, the, 102
Little Englanders, 103-9
Lloyd-George, D., 115
Lugard, Lord, 107

Macaulay, Lord, 70, 121
Macdonald, Sir J., 65, 87, 89
Madras, 21
Majuba, 80

INDEX

Malaya, 132–3
Malta, 111, 117
Manitoba, 90
Manson, Sir P., 100
Maoris, the, 93; Wars, 85, 91
Marathas, 69
Maryland, 21
Massachusetts, 21, 26
Mauritius, 69, 135
Mediterranean islands, 111
Migration, 4–7, 49–54, 82–3
Mill, J. S., 45
Milton, J., 1
Missions, 12–13, 27, 44
Mysore, 69

Nana Sahib, 73
Napoleon III, 63
Naval Limitations Treaty, 117
Navy and sea-power, 35, 115, 118
New England, 23, 31
Newfoundland, 4, 7, 19–21, 28, 135
New South Wales, 37, 44
New Zealand, 7, 44, 51–6, 91, 93
Nigeria, 100, 107
Nova Scotia, 28, 33–4

Orange Free State, 77–8, 82
Oudh, 73

Pennsylvania, 24
Pidgin-English, 11
Pilgrim Fathers, 21
Pitt, William, 38–9
Plate, River, 37
Population movements, 4–7, 49–55
Portuguese explorers, 18

Protectorates, 106
Punjab, 72

Railways, 62–4
Rajput states, 69
Raleigh, Sir W., 19
Revolution of 1688, 24–5; American, 29–31
Rhodes, Cecil, 81, 94, 96, 98–9
Rhodesia, 81
Rosebery, Lord, 3
Ross, Sir Ronald, 100

Saint Helena, 135
Scottish emigrants, 32, 50–2
Seeley, Sir J. R., 121–2
Self-government, 47
Seven Years War, 110
Shakespeare, 136
Shaw, Bernard, 3, 131
Sikhs, the, 72, 74
Singapore, 17, 117
Slavery, 27, 40–3
Smith, Adam, 35
Smith, Captain John, 21–2
Smuts, J. C., 7, 124, 127
South Africa, 7, 14, 77–83, 95–8
Spanish Main, 28
Statute of Westminster, 13, 123
Stephen, Sir J., 40, 44
Suez Canal, 112, 117
Surat, 21
Syria, 114–15

Trade, Acts of, 2, 32
Trade or Plantations, 26–7
Transvaal, 80–2
Travancore, 69
Trevelyan, Sir G. O., 103

Tropical medicine, 6, 100
Turkey, 113

Uitlanders, the, 96
Ulster, 128
Utrecht, Treaty of, 28

Victoria, Queen, 16
Victoria (Australia), 55-6

Virginia, 20, 31, 128

Wakefield, E. G., 45-7, 53
Washington, George, 29
Western Australia, 99
West Indies, 7, 21-2, 39, 133
White Man's Country, 5, 134

Zionism, 116